Buy, sell &
move house

'Buying and selling a property can be a complex and stressful experience. The trick to a smooth move is choosing the right people to help you and putting plenty of time aside to get all the jobs done.'

Kate Faulkner

About the author

Kate Faulkner has bought and sold properties personally and professionally for over 20 years. She runs www.designsonproperty.co.uk, which gives independent help and guidance to consumers, and is a consultant to the property industry to help them improve their consumer products and services. Kate is the author of three other Which? property books.

Buy, sell & move house

Kate Faulkner

This edition is for my Mum. Whatever I do, wherever I am, she's always there to lend a helping hand.

Which? Books are commissioned and published by Which? Ltd,
2 Marylebone Road, London NW1 4DF
Email: books@which.co.uk

Distributed by Littlehampton Book Services Ltd,
Faraday Close, Durrington, Worthing, West Sussex BN13 3RB

British Library Cataloguing in Publication Data
A catalogue record for this book is available from the British Library
Copyright ©Which? Ltd 2006
First edition May 2006. Second edition August 2006.
Third edition July 2007. Fourth edition September 2008.
Fifth edition September 2010. Sixth edition September 2012.

ISBN 978 1 84490 142 5

Author's acknowledgements
My thanks go to Sean and Emma Callery, Bob Vickers, Jenni Conti, Melanie Green, Dermott Jewell, Mike Naylor, Louise Restell, Pete Tynan, Kerenza Swift and Angela Newton; Andrew Chatterton, Franklyn Financial Management Ltd; Gary Best, Best Property Services; Mark Montgomery, 1st Property Lawyers; Tom McClelland at McClelland Salter; Bill McClintock, The Property Ombudsman; David Campbell, Lindsays Solicitors; Stephen Nancarrow, New Home Advisor Ltd; Colin Strachan MRICS, Shepherd Chartered Surveyors and Sonia from CMS Estate Agents.

Additional text by: Sean Callery
Printed and bound by Charterhouse, Hatfield

Paper: Essential Velvet is an elemental chlorine free paper produced at Condát in Perigord, France, using timber from sustainably managed forests. The mill is ISO14001 and EMAS certified.

For a full list of Which? Books, please call 01903 828557, access our website at which.co.uk, or write to Littlehampton Book Services.
For other enquiries call 0800 252 100

Contents

Introduction   6

1 The property market   9
Moving facts and figures ■ Essentials of moving home

2 Assets, advisers and affordability   23
How much can you afford? ■ Choosing a mortgage ■ Getting the best mortgage ■ Mortgage problems ■ Insuring your home

3 Valuing a property   73
Understanding the market ■ Comparing property prices

4 Selling your home   89
Getting yourself ready ■ Estate agents ■ Selling your property yourself ■ Energy Performance Certificates ■ The legal process ■ Selling your home ■ Problems with your sale

5 Buying a property   123
Needs versus wants ■ Choosing your location ■ Finding a property ■ First-time buyer schemes ■ Viewing property ■ Checking out a property ■ Making your offer ■ Getting a survey

6 Managing the chain   157
Running the chain gang ■ How to manage the chain

7 Preparing for move day   165
Getting organised ■ Choosing a removals firm ■ I'm moving

8 Settling in   175
File your paperwork ■ Dealing with disputes

9 Selling and buying in Scotland   185
Selling in Scotland ■ Buying in Scotland ■ Help for those on low incomes

10 Selling and buying in Northern Ireland and Ireland   195
Selling and buying in Northern Ireland ■ Selling and buying In Ireland

Glossary   205
Useful addresses   209
Index   216

Introduction

Buying and selling property is considered one of the top three most stressful events in your life. However, with good research, planning and a 'can do' attitude, buying and selling, even in a tough market, can be rewarding.

To help reduce the potentially high stress levels, understand your local property market and make plans.

Property prices

Over the last 40 years, property prices have risen and fallen, usually in line with what's happening in the economy. Previous property price booms occurred in 1971–3, 1977–8, 1987–90 and 1998–2006 and were typically followed by recessions, including 1973–4, 1990–7 and 2007. As a result, over the last 20 years we have learnt a lot about what influences property prices. There are three main factors that cause prices to go up or down. The first is confidence in the market. If there is lots of 'good news' from the media about the economy, jobs and property prices, then people are confident to commit to buying property. Next is the availability of finance. In comparison to other recessions, in 2007 we saw how finance impacts on the property market, and prices in 2012 have fallen by up to 20 per cent in some areas. Financial constraints have further exacerbated the situation,

cutting the number of properties bought and sold by half.

The final key factor affecting prices is supply and demand for individual properties Since 2007 we have seen the economy crash, with unemployment rising and the number and types of mortgages being squeezed. For the first time since 2000, in many areas there are more properties for sale than buyers, or able, to purchase them, resulting in falling prices.

In 2009, prices began to stabilise in many areas across the UK as people withdrew their properties from the market. Many decided to rent them out instead, others just decided to stay put. Reports about the economy, jobs and property prices were pretty bad, so confidence remained low. The difference in 2009 was that although there were few buyers, there were few properties for sale too. As a result, property prices started to stabilise in areas where demand matched supply. In some areas, such as parts of Central London (which are dominated by international buyers), 2009 seems to have marked the end of their property recession. In other areas, however, such as in Northern Ireland or the North East, demand has continued to fall more than supply and the economic news is still poor there; prices in 2012 were lower than they were during 2009.

In 2010, property prices took an interesting turn mainly because the three factors that affect property prices started to impact differently, depending on the area. National average property price movements are almost irrelevant to anyone buying and selling because properties and areas have divided into three levels of performance.

Property prices recovered

At the time of going to print, in areas where there are good equity levels, such as in Kings Cross, Epsom and Harrogate, property prices are continually moving forward. In these areas, people can afford deposits of 25 per cent or more, local economies have stabilised or are recovering, and there is a continued shortage of good properties available to buy.

This helps buyer confidence as well-priced properties in good locations sell quickly; buyers have little problem accessing mortgages at good rates, and, as supply is low, buyers end up competing for the best properties, so prices rise.

Property prices stabilised

In other areas, such as Ealing, West Bridgford and Exeter, economic stability seems to have returned.

People have cash for a deposit, but as there are still a few properties for sale, prices are stabilising rather than moving forward.

Property prices falling

Unfortunately, in 2012 economic performance, unemployment levels and access to mortgage finance isn't equal across the UK. This means some areas, such as Barking, Newcastle and Newport, are still 'stuck' in the credit crunch and so far more properties are available for sale than there are buyers able to purchase. In these areas, property markets are still falling.

Selling and buying during a recession

Whatever is happening across the UK, people still need to buy and sell property. They get married, have babies or are forced to sell because of death, divorce or debt, so, during these uncertain times, it is essential you research extensively, plan your move carefully and use good local market experts.

Understand your market

This isn't just about what's happening in your town or village, it's about what's happening to the property type (character three-bed versus new build four-bed) you are looking to sell and buy. Knowing your market will help ensure you:

■ **Price your property correctly** so you secure a sale.
■ **Know what kind of offer to make** on the property you want to buy.

Check you can secure finance

Lenders are very cautious about who they give money to these days, so it is essential to check your credit rating first. If you have changed your job or perhaps become self-employed, this can affect who will lend money to you and how much you can borrow (see page 32).

You will also have to make sure you have a big enough deposit to secure a mortgage rate that enables you to afford the monthly mortgage payments now and when interest rates return to normal levels. Getting the right deal isn't as easy as it used to be, so it is essential to get expert help from an independent financial advisor and/or mortgage broker (see pages 50–8).

Price your property competitively

When selling your property (see pages 89–122), it is always tempting to put it on the market at as high a price as possible. However, when there aren't huge numbers of buyers out there, it is worth considering pricing your property competitively. This should generate more viewings, which, in turn, should lead to more offers – and the best way to secure the top price for your property is to have two or more people competing for it.

Be aware of changing circumstances

It is essential to keep your eye on things that will affect your purchase or sale, as outlined to the right.

■ What is happening to interest rates and how will this affect your affordability?

■ Are mortgage rates going up in line with interest rates, or are they going up even if interest rates stay the same? How this affects you will partly depend on the mortgage you have, so check with your mortgage adviser.

■ Make sure you have a back-up plan should things go wrong. For example, life changes such as unemployment, sickness and financial difficulties do happen, so ensure you have a way of surviving these things, just in case (see pages 48–9 and 61–3).

■ Think through how long you are intending to stay in the property. For those who bought just before the recession in the 1990s, some properties took five or more years to recover their previous value. So if you are thinking of buying and moving again within five years, make sure you have some contingency plans in place – just in case your property doesn't go up in price, or worse still, falls (see pages 24–35).

With the help of this book you can make sure that, whatever your buying and selling circumstances may be, you have support at every stage. The main part of the book deals with buying and selling in England and there are separate chapters covering Scotland (see pages 185–94) and Northern Ireland and Ireland (see pages 195–204).

The property market

1

Property is big business, and nearly all of us get involved in the market sometime – with varying degrees of enthusiasm. This chapter gives an overview of the market, introduces the essential information and explains the likely timescales involved. It also explains the importance of new laws.

Moving facts and figures

Rises and falls in house prices regularly feature in news reports, and most newspapers (both national and local) run substantial specialist sections on the subject.

Few dinner parties finish without some reference to it, from the amazing price paid for a shell of a building to the difficulty that young people have in affording even the smallest place of their own.

There is much hype about the property market and when you are buying and selling a property it is hard to get to grips with the essential facts and figures that help to equip you for a successful move. The following information puts the house market in context and helps you to plan your move from the start.

Key figures often quoted by the media include:

- The average price of a home.
- The number of properties sold in any year.
- Whether the market is increasing or decreasing.
- Regional variations.

Historically there were up to 375,000 properties for sale at any one time. During 2008–09, however, sales volumes dropped by approximately 60 per cent, so many fewer properties were available for sale. Things have picked up since then and five years on in 2012, according to Rightmove, just over 531,000 properties were live on their site. They tend to sell within two to three months. Statistically, property prices in 2012 are static. However, this isn't really reflective of any property prices when it comes to buying and selling. In today's tough market it is essential to find out what's happening in the area that you are buying and selling in rather than rely on media headlines, which typically report national averages.

To date, we move house on average every seven years, which

 You can find current data on moving facts at these websites: **www.landregistry.gov.uk; www.hometrack.co.uk; www.rics.org** and **www.zoopla.com**. There is also additional information on relevant pages throughout this book.

- **House prices** have risen faster than wages, putting more properties out of their range.
- **The abolition of tax relief** on mortgages in 2000 increased the real cost of a mortgage.
- **Many graduates** leave university with a hefty student loan to repay, reducing the amount of money they have available for property.
- **Property investors** have continued to snap up similar properties to first-time buyers, maintaining house price levels.

Although there is conflicting information in the media, according to the Council of Mortgage Lenders, the average age of a first-time buyer has remained at 29 years since 2005. The average deposit is 20 per cent and a mortgage advance of £116,500. These changes often require first-time buyers to:

- **Accept financial help** from their family towards their deposits.
- **Use their parents** as **guarantors** on the loan.
- **Share mortgages,** sometimes with as many as four people contributing to a purchase.
- **Opt for cheaper,** smaller properties with little or no garden.
- **Go to lenders** or apply for affordable home ownership schemes offering first-time buyers a deposit of 10 per cent or less and part property ownership.

Increasingly, those that are eligible also have access to

is when most of us take an active interest in the market, but like it or not, all home owners need the property market to stay healthy. For this to happen, we are reliant on a steady flow of first-time buyers to fuel the market in the first place. So when you are looking to buy or sell a property, it is crucial to understand whether first-time buyers are active as they will influence the market in general. This is why it is vital for you to understand the impact of the local market on your buying and selling decisions (see Chapter 3, pages 79–82).

First-time buyers

Traditionally, first-time buyers have been vital to the health of the property market because they are the start of nearly every chain of purchases. The following factors make it increasingly difficult for first-time buyers to get on to the property ladder:

How many?

Over the past few years, first-time buyers have found it tough to secure finance and have been nervous to buy during times of economic uncertainty. According to the Council of Mortgage Lenders, in 2006 there were just over 400,000 first-time buyers; in 2007, 360,000 and, by 2009, 196,600. The number rose slightly in 2010 to 198,500, but dropped back to 193,000 in 2011.

The fall in first-time buyers isn't just due to price rises or lending problems. Over the last 10 years, few people have saved for a 'rainy day' or, in the case of first-time buyers, a deposit. Added to this are the expectations of first-time buyers. Many current home owners bought small properties in areas which were not great to live in but were cheap. Many first-time buyers find they can afford to rent a brand-new flat in a great location which they could not afford to buy in – and prefer to do so.

'affordable home ownership' homes, which are being built in local areas by housing associations or developers (see page 60).

Because first-time buyers are particularly crucial to the state of the market, research them when you value your property. If there are plenty of first-time buyers, the market is buoyant. A shortage of them quietens the market.

Types of property

Driving around the UK reveals the wide range of house styles that have been built over the centuries, sometimes side by side. There really is something to suit everybody (although it might not be on the market in the right location at the right price at the right time when you are looking for it!). Older, 'character' properties are especially popular and in short supply, so they command a higher price.

Thinking about the type(s) of property you are looking to buy is important. Some properties sell more quickly than others. All properties have advantages and disadvantages. Some people spend months searching for a type of property only to find that it doesn't exist in the area they want or that it is way beyond what they can afford, or other people's offers get accepted first as they are cash buyers.

For more information on the different types of property that are available see pages 125–7. Each property has their advantages and disadvantages and it is up to you to decide what you want from your new home.

Essentials of moving home

Exciting, stressful, expensive, life-affirming, worrying, exhausting ... the list of adjectives people use to describe moving house is long and often contradictory.

Without careful planning and an understanding of your own property market, it can be all of the things described above and more, so it is vital that you are sure you really do want to move house, especially if you are selling up too.

A government survey discovered that an amazing third of all property buyers pull out of the purchase process after making an offer, often wreaking havoc on their own lives and on those of the sellers, buyer and (unpaid) agents up and down the chain.

Reasons to move

People move to new properties for many reasons, which generally boil down to a change in the required size of home or location, or a change of lifestyle.

Space

New babies or new partners help to push the property market along. As people start living together, or start a family, or begin to work from home, they need more room. They might need additional space for bedrooms, offices, storage for

---

Jargon buster

Chain When there are more than two properties aiming to complete a sale on the same day.

Completion The final part of the transaction when the property title is legally given to the new owner.

Energy Performance Certificates Since 2007 it has been mandatory to have your property's energy efficiency rating assessed (see pages 105-7).

Exchange of contracts A binding legal agreement that confirms the intention to transfer ownership of a property between a buyer and seller.

Planning permission When permission has to be sought from the local council for changes that the owner would like to be make to a property.

Sale contract Contract with an estate agent (see pages 100-1).

Search Information on planning and environmental matters obtained from the local authority (see pages 147-9 for more information).

all their possessions or to improve their quality of life in some other particular way.

However, if you like where you live now, it is worth considering whether you would be able to extend your current home to provide the space you need with a new bathroom, bedroom or study. Maybe you can convert a loft into fresh living space or extend into your garden with a new living room or a conservatory? It is likely to be less stressful, and improving rather than moving gives you a chance to create the home of your dreams – but remember that your plans may be subject to planning permission.

Conversely, the other major reason why people move house is to downsize. The 'empty nesters' whose children have left home can find themselves rattling around a house that has too much space, and decide to downsize, freeing up equity to splash out on a cruise, safari or help with the kids' education.

'A third of all property buyers pull out of the purchase process after making an offer, affecting sellers and buyers along the chain.'

New job

Commuting is hard work on our congested roads and transport system, and many people would agree that a shorter daily journey time improves their quality of life. So a new job further from home or in a completely different area may mean you have to move, or buy or rent somewhere to stay during the week. If you have the resources and take a job far away, renting a room or flat to stay in on weekdays can be a good compromise at first and a fine way to discover if you like the area you intend moving to.

New location

The debate between contrasting styles of town and country life has been going on for centuries. Some people live in one and yearn for the other, others wouldn't switch for the world, and the well-heeled have a home in each. Maybe you want to move locally to be nearer friends or family, or to be in the catchment area for a school you value. Similarly, divorce, separation, redundancy or bad luck can stimulate a move to a cheaper location or a smaller home. Perhaps you just fancy a change of scenery and culture. Britain is a wonderfully varied country with much to offer in every region. Sometimes people just need a change.

The cost of moving is far from cheap. Chapter 2, starting on page 23, explains what is involved financially, both in the short term (e.g. conveyancing, furniture movers) and the long term (e.g. mortgage, running costs).

New style

For many of us, where we live represents who we are, and as we become more affluent, we want a home that reflects our station in life. An alternative is to renovate or redecorate – a new kitchen or bathroom, or even just new furniture can really lift the look of a home. All these options can transform a house and add to its value.

Time to get on the property ladder

UK property prices rose rapidly from 2000 to 2007. They fell back by up to 20 per cent in 2009 and rose once more through 2010. Depending on the area, since then prices are either rising, stable or continuing to fall.

Making the decision to buy or continue staying at home or renting can be a tough one when the market is so confusing and economic stability far from being assured. It is therefore worth answering the following questions to help with your decision-making:

1 Can you raise a deposit of between 5 and 25 per cent of the price of a home you want to buy?

2 Is a mortgage lender willing to lend the money that you need to purchase a home?

3 After buying, would you have spare monies to fund your mortgage if you were sick or lost your job? Alternatively, could you rent your property out to cover your costs?

Ideally you would also want to ensure you could stay in your property and cover all the costs for at least five years to allow prices to increase so you hopefully don't end up losing money if property prices fell further.

Reasons not to move

Selling, buying and moving to a new property soaks up a lot of money, often in addition to the costs of a bigger mortgage. You may well need to save money in order to finance costs such as stamp duty, estate agents, solicitors and removals.

It is also easy to underestimate the emotional links you can feel with a house. It may be the place where you brought up children, or met your partner, or that it has countless tiny connections that comfort you and make you feel part of it.

But the major reason to stay is that even the smoothest of house moves can be stressful and disruptive to the rhythm of your life. Bear in mind that changing where you live can be tiring in many ways: emotionally, mentally and physically – there's a lot to get through! If you can face that because what is at the other end of the road is worth it, then go ahead, but remember that the journey is rarely without hitches.

Finally, are you being realistic in your desire to move? It's only worth buying or moving if it will improve your quality of life. Have you got the funds or a likely selling

> **'The more you understand the issues you face when moving house, the easier it is to overcome them, which is what this book is designed to help.'**

price sufficient to buy what you want (for more information, see pages 24–35)?

The more you understand the issues you face, the easier it is to overcome them, which is what this book is designed to help.

Move or improve?

If you are thinking about moving for extra space, check first whether you can create the space in your current home and compare the costs of improving versus moving. For example, if you are selling your property for £150,000 and buying your next property for £260,000, it will cost you around £13,000. For this amount, you could convert a garage into a new room for approximately £9,000 and even add a small extension for £12,000. If you are at the top end of the market, and you are selling your property for say £350,000 and buying your next property for £550,000, it will

cost you around £33,000 to buy and sell. For this amount, you could convert your loft space, which could give you the extra space you need without moving at all.

The costs quoted are based on averages and will vary depending on the type of property and the location. When considering building work, always arrange a bespoke quote from a qualified builder and also check what planning permission you need to obtain first.

How long will it take?

Many of us have heard horror stories of how long a house purchase can take, and amazing tales of very rapid successes. Key factors influencing the time span include the size of the chain and the state of the market (falling prices mean slower movement). The average time taken from starting to house hunt to exchanging contracts is approximately 22 weeks. A typical move can be broken down into the following time frames:

- **From beginning to look to offer being accepted:** 12 weeks.
- **From offer acceptance to mortgage offer:** 4 weeks.
- **From mortgage offer to exchange of contracts:** 4 weeks.
- **From exchange of contracts to completion:** 2 or more weeks.

The chain of events for selling and buying a property is lengthy. For an overview of both processes, see the flow charts on pages 18-19, which are designed to help you on your way.

rapid movement involves quick decision making, which is not always best because we are not fully aware of all the implications of a decision, and feeling rushed into making important choices at this emotionally fragile time can be exceedingly stressful.

Deciding to move

It can take some months for people to decide they want to move. This doesn't tend to be a smooth process as people may start looking for a property before they put their own up for sale, adding themselves to estate agent's mailing lists. They then either see a property they want, or decide that they are definitely going to move so put their home on the market.

This process is frequently interrupted by other events, for example, someone may fall ill for a few weeks or be particularly busy at work. As a result, they dip out of the market for a while, then come back in again at a later date, or drop out completely.

Remember that this is an average of completed sales (about 28 per cent never make it to completion) and there will be plenty that took less time and many that dragged on for month after month, especially if the property for sale was priced too high. In approximately one in ten cases it takes more than 20 weeks from agreeing an offer to exchanging contracts.

As a rough guide, then, the whole process of buying a house should take between three and six months. Buying and selling is likely to extend this to six to twelve months (with the time to sell the average house being about eight or more weeks). However, there are occasions when the whole process has been completed in as little as six weeks. That said,

Putting your property up for sale

This should be a fairly quick process. The agent needs to take some measurements of your home, which they often do when valuing your property. They may send someone separately to take photos and do floor plans, and you need to agree the contract of sale and confirm the details produced on your behalf.

'**The process of buying a house can take three to six months.**'

The property procedure

There's more to dealing in property than looking in agents' windows. The key phases are set out below. Sometimes two or more can be happening simultaneously, but it still helps to know where you are in the whole procedure, what happens next, and what you might have missed. All these stages are explained in detail on the pages stated.

Selling

Decide to move

Do you really want to?
See page 90.

↓

Carry out repairs

Get it looking its best.
See pages 114–15.

↓

Research the local market

Find out what your property
might be worth. See pages 79–82.

↓

Select a legal company

Have a legal representative
ready and prepare your
paperwork. See pages 108–13.

↓

**Choose an agent and
order an EPC**

The right one will sell your home
efficiently, or can you do it?
See pages 95–100 and 103–4.

↓

Prepare your home

Clear clutter and create space.
See page 115.

Market the property

Issue particulars and spread the
word. See page 104.

↓

Guide viewers

Don't say 'This is the lounge.'
See pages 115–18.

↓

Deal with offers

Is the buyer serious?
See page 118.

↓

Agree a price

What will you accept?
See pages 86–8.

↓

Conveyancing

Make it legal and agree what's
included. See pages 109–11.

↓

Exchange contracts

Finalise the sale.
See pages 111–12.

↓

Complete contracts

Start packing the lorry.
See pages 163–4.

Buying

The affordability test

How much can you pay?
See pages 24–35.

↓

Map it out

Arrange a Mortgage Agreement
in Principle. See page 40.

↓

Choose your property type

What do you need?
See pages 124–6.

↓

Research the market

What's available, and what's
selling? See pages 135–8.

↓

Where?

Where are your property types?
See pages 133–4.

↓

Brief agents

Make your needs and wants
clear. See pages 135–6.

↓

Sort out a legal representative

Do it now so that you can move
fast if need be. See pages 108–9.

↓

View properties

Could you live there?
See pages 142–6.

Negotiate a price

What's it worth?
See page 152.

↓

Confirm your mortgage

Make sure the product is still
available and you can afford it.
See pages 36–56.

↓

Survey

Get one done.
See pages 153–4.

↓

What's included?

Sort out fixtures and fittings.
See pages 110–11.

↓

Conveyancing

Make time to check all is well.
See pages 161–2.

↓

Who's going to move you?

Choose how you will move.
See pages 166–9.

↓

Exchange contracts

Now you're committed to the
purchase. See pages 162–3.

↓

Complete

Pay the money and move in.
See pages 163–4.

↓

Register your property

Make it yours and pay the stamp
duty. See page 177.

Selling a property

As a rough guide you can expect to receive an offer when ten people have viewed your home, which could take weeks or months. You may choose not to accept their first offer, and negotiations might continue for a week or so.

Finding a property

Much depends here on how much you want to move, how realistic your expectations are and what is on the market. Having a buyer for your own property already is a powerful incentive for many to accept your offer rather than someone else's if it is a property much in demand.

Buying a property

The tasks of getting a survey done, arranging a mortgage on the property, carrying out legal searches and finalising the legal documents can overlap. But the time it takes to buy a property rests on many parties. You and the people selling the property need to get all the documentation ready quickly. The legal companies have to be ones that are happy to work to your deadlines, and the mortgage company will always want to know more information before they release tens of thousands of pounds to you.

Chain pain

The length or complexity of the chain (i.e. how many people are linked in a series of sales and purchases) is certainly a factor in the length of time that it takes to complete a sale, but a short chain can take ages if the people buying and selling, and the professionals involved, don't keep it moving.

The trouble with a chain is that everyone in it must exchange contracts on the same day, having completed all the legal and financial paperwork. This involves many people (conveyancers, mortgage lenders, estate agents, surveyors …), most of whom you have no contact with (and no control over) because they're not working for you. You can influence this by making sure anyone acting for you is professional and efficient – and can work to deadlines you set, or even by approaching the task as a project and managing it yourself (see pages 103–4 and 110).

Keeping things moving

Whether you are buying, selling or both, there is a lot you can do to help keep things moving as fast as possible:

- **Specify a time frame** when agreeing the sale and purchase deals – then everyone knows what is required of them.
- **Draw up draft sale contracts** when you put your property on the market.
- **Sort out your mortgage in principle** before looking for properties.
- **Fill in all information forms** as soon as you get them.
- **Book your surveyor** within a week of having an offer

accepted, and ensure that your legal company works as fast as possible.

- **Deliver paperwork** direct locally, and use a next-day delivery service for other written communication.
- **Specify a minimum of two weeks** between exchange and completion, four weeks if you can.
- **One or more of the parties** could agree to move to rented or temporary accommodation on a set date to free up a property in the chain, reducing the number of contracts to be exchanged on the same day.
- **Maintain a dialogue** with the estate agents along the chain – you can't speak to other people's legal representatives, but a good estate agent will be able to hurry things along and keep communication active, and it is very much in their interests to do this as they don't get paid until the property is sold.

What's new?

Over the last ten years there have been substantial changes in buying and selling a property. These range from how you search for a property through to what checks you should make when buying one. Whether you have moved in the last few years or haven't moved for a long time, there are likely to be things you will need to do that you didn't have to do last time. Here is a list of the main changes, further details are given in the relevant chapters.

The internet

Most buyers now start their property search by using property portals on the internet or estate agent websites. For sellers this means that the price you pitch your property at is important. If buyers tend to purchase in a range of £100,000–150,000 and your property is priced at £160,000 but the agent has recommended accepting any offers from £150,000, your property might be missed.

It also makes it essential to ensure photos show your property in the best light. If it is home for a family, for example, photos of lots of steps may stop people viewing.

Buyers typically divide into two types: perfect property hunters, who don't want to do anything to their new home, and wreck finders, who want a property that needs work, so they can add value. So make sure your property photos reflect what people are looking for.

For buyers, beware the internet! Deciding whether to visit a property just based on what you see online is a bad idea as the property might be different when you view it. Ideally,

Chapter 4 (pages 89-122) covers all that you need to know about the process of selling your home, and Chapter 5 (pages 123-56), likewise looks at what you should know about buying a property.

visit lots of properties for sale and get to know the streets at the start of your search. Visit properties on a bike or walk as this will give you a better feel for whether this is somewhere you want to live. Use the internet only for new properties coming onto the market. Take a quick peek from the outside and then decide if you want to visit it or not.

No sale, no fee and fixed fee conveyancing

This change means that you pay a fixed fee agreed upfront and if your sale falls through, you don't have to pay the legal fee. You do, however, still have to pay any charges, such as searches.

Delays in making offers

People tend to wait to make offers until they have sold/got an offer on their own property. This makes it more likely that their offer will actually be serious and will come to fruition.

Mortgages and insurance

You can get a 'mortgage agreement in principle', which will show sellers you can afford their property. However, mortgage costs, such as administration or booking charges, have increased dramatically and some lenders will even charge you an administration fee if you choose not to take out their building insurance.

Gas and electric checks

With changes to the regulations on property improvement (such as a new boiler or electrical works), as sellers you will need to provide a certificate of recent works you have had done. Ideally, when buying, get a gas and electrical safety certificate to reassure you that the home is safe to live in.

Proof of identity

You now need to provide the agent with proof of identity. You also need to provide your solicitor with the same thing, for example your passport.

Stamp Duty Land Tax

Stamp Duty Land Tax (SDLT) rate changes can be made every year, so it's essential to keep up with the current rates after each budget. At the time of going to print, these are the SDLT rules that are applied to the selling price of any property:

Up to £125,000	no SDLT
Over £125,000 to £250,000	1 per cent
Over £250,000 to £500,000	3 per cent
Over £500,000 to £1 million	4 per cent
Over £1 million to £2 million	5 per cent
Over £2 million	7 per cent

If the property is in a 'disadvantaged' area, there is no SDLT payable up to £150,000. Under the coalition government, properties over £2 million now attract a 7 per cent SDLT and anyone buying a property for over £2 million via a corporate body is charged 15 per cent. For the latest SDLT rates, visit www.hmrc.gov.uk/sdlt/rates-tables.htm.

Assets, advisers and affordability

2

This is the reality check: what can you actually, realistically, afford to pay for your new property? This chapter gives advice on how to assess your own finances before entering the mortgage minefield. It takes you through the process of selecting a loan and explains the other, often hidden financial implications of owning property.

How much can you afford?

Before finding your dream home, you need to make sure you can afford to buy and run it. It is surprising just how many people get to the stage of making an offer on a house before realising that they can't actually pay for it.

Sadly, by doing this, they waste their own and, perhaps more importantly, other people's time, too. Worse still, if you take on a mortgage that you can't afford and end up in arrears, you may have a repossession order to cope with and financial trouble for many years, so think very hard before you stretch yourself for that 'dream property'. For a full understanding of what you can afford, you first need to have a good grasp of your assets and liabilities.

Check regulations!

The information in this book is for guidance only and does not constitute advice, which is best obtained from an independent mortgage adviser or an independent financial adviser (IFA) who specialises in mortgages and finance. Always check that anyone you speak to is regulated by the FSA (FCA from 2013, see opposite) by going to www.fsa.gov.uk.

Assets

Your assets are all the money that you own. Including:

Value of your property

If you already own a home that you are selling, calculate the equity you will be able to carry over. This is the difference between what you owe on your current mortgage loan (a liability), and what your home is likely to sell for.

> '**Think very hard before you stretch yourself for that 'dream property'. If you end up in arrears, you may have financial trouble for the rest of your life.**'

For further analysis of your assets and liabilities, see information on income and expenditure on pages 26-7. The different types of mortgage that are available are covered on pages 36-49 and getting the right mortgage is covered on pages 50-8.

BE CAREFUL!

In 2013, the Financial Services Authority (FSA) is being disbanded and replaced with the Financial Conduct Authority (FCA). It's job is to protect consumers, enhance the integrity of the UK financial system and promote effective competition in the interests of consumers. It will also maintain a register of all the authorised financial firms and approved individuals.

Savings in bank or building society

If you have savings that you can cash, these could allow you to pay a higher deposit on your next property (see page 29), increasing the price you can afford and giving you a wider range of mortgage options.

Shares or other investments

Investment income is not usually included in mortgage calculations because it is not guaranteed. But if you have any, you could sell some investments to raise the deposit.

■ **Make sure** you know the lead time to convert these into cash. Remember that if you are paying a deposit, it needs to be paid at the time of **exchange** of contract, so you may need to raise extra cash rather than relying on the equity in your property to pay for it.

■ **Always consult** an independent financial adviser on the implications of cashing in or using any savings or investments. Think carefully before cashing in savings and investments to buy a property. You should always keep at least three months' salary as an emergency fund.

Liabilities

Your liabilities are:

Mortgage outstanding

This is the amount that is left to be paid on your mortgage. This will depend on the type of mortgage (see pages 42–7) and how long you have had it. Your lender will be able to tell you this figure.

Existing loans

These are any current debts, such as a car loan, hire purchase agreement or a large credit card debt. They may affect your ability to pay a mortgage and the offer that you make.

Assets and liabilites	
Assets	**Liabilities**
■ Value of your property	■ Mortgage outstanding
■ Savings in bank or building society that can be cashed	■ Debts, such as loans (car or hire purchase items)
■ Share or other investments that can be cashed	■ Cost of moving

Assets and liabilites: an example	
Assets	
Value of your property	£150,000
Savings in bank or building society	£5,000
Shares or other investments	£3,000
Total:	£158,000
Liabilities	
Mortgage outstanding	£120,000
Debts, such as loans	£10,000
Cost of moving	£6,000
Total:	£136,000
Net cash available (assets less liabilities):	£22,000

Cost of moving

There are many costs associated with buying, selling and moving (see pages 30–1) and you will need to include these in your calculations.

In the example calculation given above, the balance between assets and liabilities is £22,000. Some of this could become the deposit you pay on your new property, reducing the amount you need to borrow (see page 29). It can also help give you a financial cushion if you find a property you love and need to accept a lower price on your property.

(see pages 30–1)
(see page 29)

Changes in your income

You may be due a rise in salary, or if you are paid commission, bonuses or a high proportion of overtime, you may expect your actual income to go up or down in the near future. It is vital to be realistic about these figures or you may overstretch yourself and risk being unable to afford your mortgage.

Income and expenditure

Now you know your assets and liabilities, you can make a deeper study of your income and expenditure to help you decide how much mortgage you can afford and how much you will need to run a new property.

Income

Income is the money you earn. Gross income is your earnings before tax and other deductions, after which it is known as net income. Your lender is only likely to count half of income such as overtime, commission or bonuses unless it is guaranteed. You can check (and prove!) your income with your three most recent payslips or the P60 form that is issued each year in April. The P60 gives details of your pay and how much tax has been deducted.

Expenditure

Expenditure is the payments you make, from a chocolate bar paid for with small change to buying a car or paying the monthly insurance premium. You don't need to be aware of every single purchase, but you do need to know how much you spend each month and what it goes on. Make an honest list of your monthly expenses by checking through your bank and credit card statements. This will tell you how much you're spending on the categories outlined in the table opposite. Keep a note of this figure for later in this chapter. Next it is important to be aware of the cost of buying a home.

Monthly expenditure

Use this list as the basis of your calculations for your monthly expenditure. Be honest!

Food and drink £ _____

Clothes £ _____

Household items £ _____

Telecom charges £ _____
- mobile
- landline/internet

TV expenses £ _____
- licence
- digital channels

Fuel £ _____
- oil
- gas
- electricity

School expenses £ _____

Car and travel £ _____
- loan
- fuel
- tax
- servicing
- train/bus/underground

Entertainment £ _____

Holidays £ _____

Subscriptions £ _____

Standing orders and direct debits £ _____

Insurances £ _____
- car
- building
- house contents

Water rates £ _____

Council Tax £ _____

Loan and hire purchase repayments £ _____

Other £ _____

Costs of buying

Buying a property doesn't just mean getting a mortgage and finding somewhere you like. You also need to set money aside for the many costs associated with selling, buying and moving. The chart overleaf outlines the different areas that you need to be aware of when making your plans – legal costs, mortgage fees and removals add up to a surprisingly large amount of money. And then there is the deposit to concern yourself with.

New house, new bills

When looking into the costs of buying, you must also allow for any expenses that would be significantly different in a new home. For example:

- Your new property might be in a higher Council Tax band, or in a region with higher Council Tax levels. Your commuting costs may also be higher.

- Larger houses cost more to run. For example, your utility bills may vary:

1-bedroom flat	£750* per annum
2-bedroom terrace	£900* per annum
3-bedroom semi-detached	£1,150* per annum
4-bedroom detached	£2,000* per annum
5- to 5-bedroom+ detached	£2,500–3,350* per annum

* Based on lowest cost utility companies, paying by direct debit for joint gas and electricity for two people for flats and terraces and four people for three-bedroomed semis and above.

Jargon buster

Arrangement fee A fee charged by some lenders on particular deals.
County Court Judgement (CCJ) A judgement for a debt that is made by the county court.
Deposit The down payment on a property, which is paid when contracts are exchanged.
Equity The difference between the price of a property sold and the loan on it.
Exchange of contracts A binding legal agreement that confirms the intention to transfer ownership of a property between a buyer and seller.
Higher lending charge premium The payment that needs to be made for a higher lending charge (see page 48 for more information).
Survey A report on the condition of a property.

The deposit

The deposit is the cash down payment you make on your new home. The larger your deposit, the better interest rates you are likely to have access to on your mortgage, so it is worth considering paying what you can afford. When you have a large deposit (more than 10 per cent), you'll also normally avoid the possibility of a higher lending charge. These charges can be several hundreds of pounds or even £2,000–£3,000, depending on the price of the property.

In the past, some mortgage companies would offer 100 per cent mortgages, removing the need to have a deposit to buy a property. However, with the recession hitting hard and property prices stagnating, 100 per cent mortgages are now too risky for lenders so they have been pulled in most cases (see also the advice given on higher lending charges on page 48).

Thanks, mum and dad

An increasing social trend is for parents or grandparents to gift or loan money to their offspring so that they can buy their first home. On average they lend or give £18,000 if they can afford it – and some relatives even take on a loan themselves to achieve this.

The low-down on deposits

Buyers are usually expected by the vendor and their legal company (solicitor and/or conveyancer) to pay a 5 per cent deposit on properties under £99,999 at time of exchange (which means a £90,000 house requires a £4,500 deposit) and 10 per cent for those costing more than this (so on a £200,000 home it would be £20,000), although this can vary. The amount of initial deposit you pay is subject to an agreement between the buyer and seller via the solicitor. When trading down, you can use the money from your buyer's deposit to put down on your next house.

A few lenders will offer up to 95 per cent of the value, especially on NewBuy schemes, but this is not always the case. For example, some mortgage lenders don't lend on timber or thatched properties. So be aware that it is not just your ability to make a certain level of mortgage payments that determines your mortgage offer, it also depends on the type and age of a property, its condition and other factors, which are discussed on pages 61 and 147–51.

There are a few websites with budget planners to help you with your calculations: **www.designsonproperty.co.uk** and **www.1stpropertylawyers.co.uk**.

Costs of buying and moving home

Use this table to give you an approximate idea of the costs of buying and moving home. Select the relevant figures for legal, mortgage and removals costs and then add together for the total cost. If you are selling, take the value of your property and multiply it by 1.8 per cent to gain an idea of the fee you are likely to have to pay to an estate agent.

	Value of property				
	Up to £99k	£100–£249k	£250–350k	£401–£450k	£501k+
Legal costs					
Fees	300	400	400	450	600
Searches	200	200	200	200	200
Stamp duty	see ready reckoner				
Money transfer	36	36	36	36	36
Land Registry fee	130	280	280	280	550
Leasehold♦	122	122	122	122	122
Sub-total					

	Value of property				
	Up to £99k	£100–£249k	£250–350k	£401–£450k	£501k+
Mortgage and survey costs					
Valuation	250	350	375	450	500
Arrangement fee▲ And/or booking fee	900	950	1,000	1,000	1,000
Higher lending charge●	For guidance, see www.designsonproperty.co.uk				
Survey fee■ – Either homebuyer – Or building	300 500	400 600	500 800	600 900	800 1,300
Sub-total					

	Number of bedrooms				
	1 bedroom	2 bedrooms	3 bedrooms	4 bedrooms	5 bedrooms
Removals					
Hire a van	100	200	Not Recommended	Not Recommended	Not Recommended
Removal company	400	500	800	1,000	1,200+
Add packing by removal company	150	200	250	350	400
Sub-total					
Total					

* Only add this figure if you are buying a property that is leasehold.
▲ If you are obtaining a mortgage, check whether you need to pay an arrangement and/or booking fee (see page 51).
• A higher lending charge is only appropriate in certain cases – see the website shown on the table and also page 48.
■ The choice of survey is yours to make – for information, see pages 153–4.

Stamp duty land tax ready reckoner

The current (April 2012) SDLT rates are:

Property value	Stamp duty
Up to £125,000	Nil
Over £125,000 to £250,000	1%
Over £250,000 to £500,000	3%
Over £500,000 to £1 million	4%
Over £1 million to £2 million	5%
Over £2 million	7%

For the latest SDLT rates, visit www.hmrc.gov.uk/sdlt/intro/rates-thresholds.htm.

Other factors

Other things that can affect how much lenders will offer you, and therefore how much you can afford to spend, include:

Credit worthiness

Anyone who lends you money will assess your credit worthiness. Lenders do this by checking your credit file. This is a record of your financial history together with other information, such as details of any bankruptcies and **County Court Judgements** (CCJs). Lenders will assess this information together with the details you provided on your application form and any information they already hold on you. Lenders use different methods of assessing you, so you may be rejected by one and accepted by another.

If you find you're refused credit by mainstream lenders, there are specialist lenders who may lend to you even though your credit history means you are a greater risk.

If you think any of the information on your credit file may be wrong, you can request a copy of your file. There are three credit reference agencies (CRAs): Equifax, Experian and Callcredit (see below). They will send you a copy of your file by post for £2. You can also obtain a copy online but charges can vary between CRAs.

If there is a mistake on your file:

- **Write to the CRA** and ask it to remove or change the entry explaining why it's wrong and sending any evidence.
- **The CRA has 28 days** to act. In the meantime, the entry is marked as disputed on your file.
- **If the CRA decides** not to make a correction, you can send it a notice of correction to be added to your file. This should explain why you think the entry is wrong and point out any mitigating circumstances.

Be sure to check your file regularly. If you do find incorrect information, you can also contact your lender or credit provider.

> '**Anyone who lends you money will assess your credit worthiness.**'

Being self-employed

You will need to provide evidence of income for the last two or three years depending on the lender because the mortgage company will treat the average profit that you pay tax on for that period as

---

If you think there may be incorrect information on your credit file, contact the three main credit checking companies. Go to websites **www.equifax.co.uk**, **www.experian.co.uk** or **www.callcredit.co.uk**.

your income. If you haven't been self-employed that long, you may have less choice of mortgages and be asked to pay a higher deposit or higher interest rate.

Not having a permanent job

If, for example, you are a contract worker, you may be asked to get a letter from your employer confirming they will continue to give you work, or to provide other evidence that your earnings will continue to be the same.

If you have ever been declared bankrupt

Buyers with these circumstances tend to be offered more expensive (i.e. higher rate) mortgages as the loan companies limit their risks. Contact an independent financial adviser for help.

Joint mortgages

Unmarried couples are usually treated the same as a husband and wife in working out how much they can borrow. Gay or lesbian couples can also apply, as well as groups of two or more friends who are combining their finances to get on the property ladder (they are known as multiple applicants, see pages 141-2). However, it may be harder for them to find a lender willing to take on the loan because if one mortgage owner moves out, the remaining person may still be responsible for all of the loan.

How much can I borrow?

The key concepts here are affordability and, due to the recession, your credit record. While the recession affects the availability of credit and the economy, you will have to work a lot harder to find the best mortgage for your needs, especially if you only have a 5–10 per cent deposit.

For the past 10 years credit was easy to find as the mortgage lenders remained confident that property prices would continue to increase. When prices are stagnating and even falling, lenders want to protect their money but many remain happy to lend to people with a good credit record and large amounts of equity in their property. That way, if property prices fall, they are more likely to get their money back if anything goes wrong.

It is important to keep a regular check of your finances – what's coming in and going out. The more you have saved for a deposit the better. The table overleaf gives two examples of annual income and expenditure. The figures used are for guidance only because affordability differs for everyone. The maximum amount you can borrow is calculated from your net income, in other words your regular salary. If your salary includes overtime, commission or bonuses, your lender is likely to have their own calculation on how much of it will count as income. However, they may look favourably on applicants

Example of annual income versus expenditure

Base your deductions on the figures from your monthly expenditure calculations (see page 27), multiplying them by 12.

	Working couple with company car and no children	Working couple with two children
Income		
Salary 1	£20,000	£20,000
Salary 2	£10,000	£10,000
Total income	£30,000	£30,000
Annual income after tax	£21,000	£21,000
Deductions		
Food and drink	£3,640	£6,240
Clothes	£800	£1,000
Household expenses♦	£1,440	£1,600
School expenses	None	£750
Car loan	None	£2,000
Fuel	None	£1,500
Entertainment/holidays	£5,000	£1,500
Subscriptions	£150	None
Standing orders and direct debits▲	£100	£50
Insurances	£300	None
Water rates	£500	£500
Council tax	£1,200	£1,000
Loan and hire purchase repayments	None	£600
Total deductions	£13,130	£16,740
Income minus deductions	£7,870	£4,260

♦ These include costs of fuel and running a telephone and television
▲ Do not include any current mortgage payments you are making in this figure

The final figure in each column shows the amount that each couple have available each year to cover a mortgage and the higher costs of running a larger home. Clearly the first couple can afford much more than the second couple, even though their income is identical. This illustrates the importance of considering what you can afford rather than just working from multiples of income.

with good future prospects of a secure, high income such as doctors, accountants and solicitors.

Base your own calculations on the monthly expenditure table you drew up from the list on page 27.

How much can I afford?

This is the crucial question. If you are planning to start or increase the size of your family, your income will be affected. During the advice process, your broker or adviser can ask you if this is the case as it will certainly influence your ability to make the monthly payments. It is important to divulge as much information as possible to make sure you gain the best recommendation for your circumstances.

Income would also be reduced by either partner suffering long-term illness, taking a career break or re-training. In the main, mortgage rates are influenced by interest rates. If you take out a mortgage when interest rates are historically low (such as 0.5 per cent), don't forget that you need to be able to afford the mortgage payments when interest rates rise back to 5–7 per cent – or go even higher. Don't mortgage yourself to the maximum, because there is no safety margin if things go wrong, and that could cost you your home.

What can go wrong?

Paying a mortgage is a big responsibility and life changes may affect your ability to pay it. Think through these scenarios. Would you be able to manage?

Interest rates going up

This can have a dramatic impact on your monthly payments – for more information, see page 36.

Valuation lower than price

Sometimes the lender values a property at a lower figure than the agreed selling price. This could be because they have a different perspective on the local market or because they find faults with the property. You could re-negotiate the price, or you might decide that you are willing to stick to the agreed price. The difference need not be a problem if you can make it up and the lender is still happy to loan you the sum you need. It may, however, influence what level of loan you can secure.

Losing a job or income

Any change in your financial status, such as losing your job, will affect how much you can afford. You will need to discuss this with your loan provider, think carefully and decide for yourself if you still want to go ahead with the move.

There are various schemes designed to help someone who can no longer afford to pay a mortgage. Ranging from short-term measures to something more drastic, these are all covered in detail on pages 61-3.

Choosing a mortgage

Getting a mortgage is one of the biggest financial transactions of your life, which has implications on your financial well-being for decades to come.

If you choose the wrong mortgage and don't keep checking that you have the right deal for your circumstances, it could cost you tens of thousands of pounds.

Mortgage definition

A mortgage is a loan secured on a property. This means the mortgage company owns all or part of your home until you pay back the money. You can't sell it without paying off the loan. If you don't keep up the monthly payments, the lender can take possession of the home.

How repayments can vary

This table shows how monthly repayments on a £100,000 repayment mortgage over 25 years would vary with a changing interest rate.

Interest rate	Monthly payment
5%	£591.27
6%	£651.88
7%	£715.08
8%	£780.65
9%	£848.38
10%	£918.06
11%	£989.50
12%	£1,062.49

Prior to the 2007 recession there were thousands of mortgages that you could choose from and over 140 providers. Nevertheless, even though there are fewer mortgages to choose from today, it is still tricky to find the right one. So make the time to investigate mortgages prior to looking at properties, checking they are still available prior to making an offer so that you know what you can afford. This will put you in a stronger negotiating position.

Risk versus reward

Lenders used to be happy to lend as much as they could, subject to their own criteria, as that's the way they made money. However, the US subprime mortgage market problems has shown that, on occasion, lenders get the mix of risk and reward wrong. As a result, the risk they are now willing to take when lending money to buyers in the UK is a lot less than it used to be.

Typically, the higher the proportion of the loan to value of the property and how good or bad your credit rating is determines how risky the loan is. In addition, when property prices are stagnant or falling, mortgage companies are less likely to lend money and, when they do, it can be at a higher rate and requires a higher deposit.

As a borrower, the most important consideration is the effect that different interest rates have on your monthly payments (see table left). Since the last recession in the 1990s, interest rates have fluctuated around a historic low of 5–7 per cent (and as low as 0.5 per cent in 2012) with mortgage rates rising despite no interest rate changes. When considering a mortgage, think what would happen if there were more economic shocks as this could cause interest rates to rise to 10 per cent or more (as we saw in the 1990s). Check the highest interest rate payments you could afford to pay to stay in the property by using some of the online mortgage calculators given in the box at the foot of page 29. If it suits you, you could look at a fixed or capped interest rate (if available) to help avoid this problem (see pages 43–4).

On top of this, don't rely on property values always increasing – consider what would happen if they fell and you had to sell within a few years of buying.

Getting a mortgage

First, work out how much you can afford (see page 33). Get proof of your income(s), such as wage slips for the last six months or a P60 form, or a letter from your employer confirming your salary and any bonuses or commission that form part of your income and any other relevant financial information, such as life insurance, critical illness policies or income protection. Some of these may be provided by your employer.

It is well worth shopping around for your mortgage. Start by investigating online, because you can quickly change figures to see how they affect the monthly payments. Seek advice from your current lender and a mortgage broker or an independent financial adviser as you are then less likely to make an expensive mistake. There are several sources for this information.

Websites

Which? and the Government have websites containing independent information about mortgages (see the addresses below).

They also both offer a mortgage search that lets you search for mortgages with particular features. The Which? site lets you compare different mortgages based on the total cost of the mortgage.

**For information on mortgages, see the following websites:
www.direct.gov.uk, www.moneynet.co.uk,www.moneysupermarket.co.uk
and www.which.co.uk/money.**

Lenders

Banks and building societies usually recommend mortgages from their own range. If you've already got an existing mortgage, ask the lender to see what they will offer you – it's always worth trying to negotiate the best deal possible.

Intermediaries

As well as going direct to a lender you can also go to a mortgage broker or independent financial adviser to help you find a mortgage. Some of the cheapest deals are now only available directly from the lender so even if you see an intermediary, check any offers against direct to consumer deals

lenders are offering. Intermediaries may search all the mortgages they can (but won't have access to all lenders' mortgages or every deal available), which is referred to as 'whole of market', or they may only be able to offer mortgages from a selection of lenders. Some have their own deals they have negotiated with lenders, which aren't available elsewhere. They must tell you at the outset just how many lenders they are searching against.

Independent advisers must give you the choice of paying a fee for their service or relying on the commission from the lender for their income. If they take the commission option, you may still pay a fixed administration fee for the service you receive, or pay nothing at all. Any fee charged for advice is usually a percentage of the mortgage, which used to be from 0.2 to 2 per cent, but is now as much as 1 to 3 per cent. It's normally cheaper to opt for the procurement route instead of an advice fee. Typically independent brokers may also charge an 'administration fee' to process the mortgage on your behalf (as opposed to giving advice). If you use an IFA, check that they specialise in mortgages as some don't.

Jargon buster

APR Annual percentage rate - a standardised way of stating the total cost of a loan over the whole term.
Fee A cost charged direct to you by a mortgage broker or independent financial adviser, usually charged on an hourly basis.
Mortgage Conduct of Business Regulations laid down by the Financial Services Authority (FSA) (Financial Conduct Authority (FCA) from 2013, see page 25).
Procurement fee A fee that a financial adviser and mortgage brokers receive if they recommend a mortgage or policy that you then sign up for.

For more information on choosing a mortgage lender or intermediary, see pages 50-8, which describes the different levels of service and explains how you can assess what is best for you.

Your rights

In October 2004, the Financial Services Authority (FSA) took over the regulation of most mortgage sales. Until the change of the FSA to the FCA (see page 25), the Mortgage Code covers anyone involved in mortgage lending, administration or advice.

Give clear information

This relates to mortgages and mortgage services and the information must be given in a standard 'key facts' format so that it is easy to compare mortgages and services from different lenders.

Make price information obvious

All price information should appear in advertising and marketing material, including the annual percentage rate (APR), but it must be clearly laid out.

Recommend a suitable mortgage

The advice that is given must be based on your personal needs and circumstances.

Offer greater protection

Should you get into arrears with your mortgage, there are rules in place about the steps firms should take to treat you fairly.

Offer redress

If you have a dispute with your lender, you can take your complaint to the Financial Ombudsman Service. The Financial Services Compensation Scheme, which can pay compensation if a firm is unable or unlikely to be able to pay is also available to you.

BE CAREFUL!

A mortgage broker can only use the term 'independent' if they search the whole market, (although they can't access direct to consumer only deals). Advisers can suggest you pay a fee for the advice, keep the fee from the lender, or a mix of both. Make sure they advise of their charges up front prior to securing a mortgage.

Insurance companies

Life insurance companies employ salespeople who are also mortgage brokers. Like IFAs, they may or may not specialise in mortgages.

Estate agents

Some estate agents employ people in their branches who can give mortgage advice: either mortgage brokers, IFAs or life insurance representatives.

Employers such as banks and financial institutions

Sometimes companies offer competitive mortgages as a fringe benefit to their employees. Other large employers may have links to financial companies, which give preferential rates to employees. Check if these offers are available to you and what would happen if you left.

Builders or developers

Builders or developers can arrange loans as an incentive to buy their properties. This may be convenient, but check that their offer stands up against others on the market and if there are restrictions on their lending, such as high penalty

clauses. They may also offer a part-exchange deal where they buy your current home, which is worth considering if you are keen to secure a smoother move.

Getting a map

A Mortgage Agreement in Principle (MAP) is an expression of a mortgage lender's willingness to enter into an agreement subject to other conditions being met, such as full credit checks and a satisfactory property valuation. Obtaining a MAP through a lender shows you are serious about buying a property and have the finances available that you claim. This could be invaluable if you are competing with someone else for a property you both like: the seller is more likely to opt for someone who can prove their ability to afford the property. It also saves you any embarrassment of having to pull out from a deal having made an offer that you later found was more than you can afford.

A Mortgage Agreement in Principle costs nothing and are usually valid from a few days to three months. They involve checks on your credit rating, earnings and affordability. You can obtain a MAP online from many mortgage lenders in about 15 minutes, or get one from a branch of a bank or building society or an IFA, mortgage broker or other intermediary – and it is something worth doing if you are serious about buying.

If you do get a MAP, the credit search is registered on your file. The more searches registered the lower your credit rating. However, if you shop around to see what mortgage rates lenders will give you, this will not be registered as a search.

How long?

You can take out a mortgage covering any period – usually up to your retirement age as a maximum – but the standard term is 25 years. The longer the mortgage term, the less your monthly payments, but the more you will eventually pay in interest. As a result, the faster you can pay off your mortgage loan, the less interest you will pay. So in summary, taking a £100,000 loan for 15 rather than 25 years would cost more each month, but could save about £3,300 in interest over the term of the loan (see the chart below). Some key questions will help you choose.

When do you want to pay off the loan?

This will help you decide whether you are happy with the standard 25-year loan, to increase it to 30 years or reduce it to ten years, depending on what you can afford each month and when you want to be mortgage free.

> **'The faster you can pay off your loan, the less interest you will pay.'**

The costs of a repayment mortgage over different terms

This graph shows the costs of a £100,000 repayment mortgage with an interest rate of 6 per cent over five years. It demonstrates the benefits of choosing a shorter term if you can afford it. Although a shorter term means higher monthly repayments, this has the same effect as overpaying your mortgage – more of your money goes towards paying off your mortgage and less in interest.

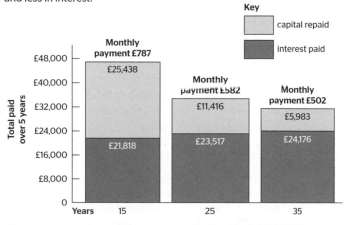

Key
- capital repaid
- interest paid

Total paid over 5 years

	15	25	35
Monthly payment	£787	£582	£502
capital repaid	£25,438	£11,416	£5,983
interest paid	£21,818	£23,517	£24,176

£48,000
£40,000
£32,000
£24,000
£16,000
£8,000
0

Years

Will you want to pay off lump sums or overpay at any stage?

The faster you pay off your mortgage, the less interest charges you pay. So if you plan to pay off your mortgage with any spare earnings or money you receive, make sure that you choose a rate and lender that will allow you to do this without any penalties. Some, for example, won't let you pay extra while you are on a special interest rate deal (such as a fixed rate). Others may limit the amount you can repay. For example, some allow you to overpay by 10 per cent of the loan value per annum. For example, if you owe £100,000 in year one, you can overpay by a maximum of £10,000, then if it drops to £85,000 in the next year, £8,500 and so on (see also page 47). Paying off your mortgage early can save you tens of thousands of pounds in interest rate payments.

Types of mortgage

It can be very confusing picking your way through the mortgage minefield, and it is certainly worth getting as much advice as you can. Everyone's finances are different and people have varying attitudes to risk, which will influence their choice of mortgage.

If you already have a mortgage, moving house is a natural time to review it, re-assessing not just the amount of your loan, but whether it is the best deal available for your current circumstances. You may find that this has changed since your current mortgage was arranged.

Starting with the basics, there are two key types of mortgage: repayment and interest only. These choices are only about how you repay your mortgage. The interest rates (there are more choices here, see pages 43–4) determine how much you pay and whether your payment will vary. It is really important to gain independent financial advice on the best way to repay your mortgage for your circumstances (see page 35).

Repayment mortgage

This means that you are paying off both the loan and the interest owed in monthly instalments. So at the end of a typical loan period of 25 years, the whole sum has been paid off and you own the property outright. Monthly payments are always higher than for interest-only loans. A repayment mortgage is the only type that guarantees you'll repay the mortgage by the end of your chosen term.

For more information on dealing with mortgage lenders and intermediaries, see pages 50–1 where matters such as the different level of service and initial disclosure documents are explained. See also www.whichmortgageadvisers.co.uk.

Interest-only mortgage

This involves paying only the interest on the loan, so after a typical loan period of 25 years, you still owe the mortgage lender the original amount you borrowed. You have to re-pay the loan amount and most borrowers pay separately into a savings or investment account to ensure they have the capital to do so. Typical investments used include an ISA or pension schemes. The aim is for them to provide you with enough to pay off the balance of the loan when the term ends. Some investment plans have not performed as well as expected in recent years, and you may be left with a shortfall, still owing the lender money. On the other hand, if the policy does well, you may have enough money to pay back the lender and have additional cash to spend too. It is your responsibility to ensure you have enough to repay the loan at the end of the mortgage.

Before you choose a mortgage, compare the total cost of each mortgage and look out for early repayment charges (see pages 47–8).

> '**The longer the mortgage term, the less your monthly payments, but the more you will eventually pay in interest.**'

Types of interest rate

There are five ways in which your interest can be applied to a mortgage. Read below and over the page.

Standard variable rate (SVR)

This is the standard product offered by lenders and is linked to the lender's cost of borrowing, plus a margin (the lender's profit!). The level of the SVR depends on the lender and there is a wide range on the market. There is also no guarantee that the SVR will move in line with bank base rate and in 2012 we saw mortgage lenders raising SVRs by 0.5 per cent or more despite interest rates remaining at 0.5 per cent.

Fixed rate

This means the interest rate stays the same for a set time (usually two to five years), whatever happens to the base rate, which is set by the Bank of England. At the end of that period, the rate typically reverts to the lender's standard variable rate. In reality, you can then re-negotiate the loan or even consider switching to another lender to get a better deal. If the variable rate falls below what you are paying during the set period, you can lose out. If it rises above your fixed rate during this period, then this type of rate works in your favour.

The main advantage of this arrangement is that you know what your monthly repayments will be for a certain number of years, allowing you to plan the rest of your finances with some security.

Assets, advisers and affordability

Capped rate

This type of deal guarantees the maximum rate you will pay for a set period (generally three to five years). If the base rate falls, so does your rate and the amount you pay. You tend to pay more for a capped rate than a fixed rate. If the rate rises, it only rises as far as the 'capped' rate. Capped rate mortgages are attractive when it is uncertain whether interest rates are likely to rise or fall. Be aware, too, that some deals have a 'collar rate', which limits how low the rate can drop, potentially reducing your benefit if the base rate falls significantly.

Discounted rate

This is a set reduction from the standard variable rate for a set period of two to five years. So if your reduction is 2 per cent and the SVR is 6 per cent, you'll pay 4 per cent – and if the lender's SVR rises to 7 per cent your rate will rise from 4 to 5 per cent, causing your monthly payments to rise too. This appeals to customers attracted by a lower rate than a fixed or capped rate and who are prepared for payments to vary. It is an attractive option when interest rates are on a downward path as the lender will have to pass on any discounts to

you. Remember, though, that the lender isn't obliged to lower its standard variable rate when the base rate falls and although they have in the past, it isn't necessarily straightaway and does not always move by the same number of percentage points.

Base rate tracker

A base rate tracker is similar to a discounted rate, but it ties your rate above or below the Bank of England base rate. So if you are on a 0.5 per cent discounted deal and the base rate is 5.5 per cent, you pay 5 per cent. Changes in the base rate affect your monthly payments – and you gain the full advantage of the drop if they fall, but similarly your rate rises with the base rate if it rises. Trackers ensure you will benefit fully if rates fall.

'**The bank base rate is set by the Bank of England – it can go up as well as down and will have a bearing on your mortgage repayments.'**

Remember that each of these different types of interest rate – and the other incentives listed on pages 45-6 – can apply to both repayment and interest-only mortgages, which were described on pages 42-3.

Combination deals

These are deals with several of the elements just described. For example, you might get a one-year fixed rate, which then turns into a two-year discount rate.

Other incentives

There are other types of deals that are marketed by mortgage lenders to try to gain your business and these can be given with any of their mortgages and interest rate deals. Before you take up any of these deals, check that it is right for you, not just in the short-term as it may cost you more money in the long run.

Cash back

This is an incentive to sign up with a lender where you get some of the loan (say 5 per cent) back in cash. This can help cover the costs of a new car or furnishing a new home when you are buying a new home, but you are likely to be tied into the lender for a period of time and may pay a higher interest rate than on other deals.

Flexible or offset mortgages

Flexible and offset mortgages offer non-standard features, which can be useful to some people in certain circumstances, although they charge a higher interest rate as a result.

A flexible mortgage allows you to increase your monthly payments and pay lump sums off your mortgage. These overpayments reduce your mortgage balance so you end up paying less interest in the long run. Some deals also allow you to borrow back any overpayments you have made, take a payment holiday or make underpayments.

If you think you're only interested in making overpayments, consider a standard mortgage instead as these tend to be cheaper and some allow overpayments. But check carefully that there aren't any restrictions on the amount you can overpay.

Flexible mortgages can also allow a 'drawdown' facility allowing you to borrow more money. For example, you might buy a property that needs some work. You think you've budgeted well for the work but you find it goes over and you need more money, often quickly! One way of doing this is to borrow more than you need and 'drawdown' the additional money if required. For example, you may need a £140,000 mortgage for the property and intend to spend £20,000 of that sum renovating. This figure then

> ### BE CAREFUL!
> Some low interest rate or cash back deals can be more expensive than they might appear because you are tied to a lender's uncompetitive rate for years, or you may be forced to take out their home insurance or payment protection policies. Beware of picking a deal that looks great in the short term, without looking at the whole cost of the loan over the period. Be aware, too, of lenders that impose early repayment charges if you switch to another provider or make early repayments.

increases to £30,000 due to costs not anticipated and changes you make in the specification. If you had taken out a £150,000 mortgage with a £10,000 'drawdown' facility, then you would be able to cover the increase in costs. But if you don't need it, you don't draw it down and hence don't pay for it. Bear in mind that the extra amount you borrow will be secured on your house along with the rest of the loan. And if you choose to spread the repayments over the usual mortgage term (25 years, say), you'll end up paying more back than if you went for a shorter term unsecured personal loan.

An offset mortgage combines your savings, and in some cases your current account, with your mortgage. In effect, your savings or account balance reduces the amount of the loan and hence cuts the interest paid on it. You can still take out your money from your savings or current account, but you will then have to pay more interest as your loan will have increased.

For example, if you have a £100,000 mortgage and have amassed savings of £10,000, you can pay this sum into a linked savings account, effectively reducing your mortgage to £90,000. So you'll pay less interest as your loan has shrunk – but you won't earn interest on your savings. The theory is that if your savings earn a lower rate of interest than what you are paying on your mortgage, you are better off using your savings to reduce your mortgage. The more money you have available to offset against the mortgage, the lower your payments will be. The arrangement is of most benefit to higher-rate tax payers with substantial savings (more than 15 per cent of the value of the mortgage).

These are complex arrangements requiring careful monitoring, so it is vital to get independent mortgage advice before taking on this or any type of mortgage.

Self-certification mortgage

If you are self-employed, it can be difficult to secure a mortgage. You have to prove your income via your accounts and this may vary dramatically throughout the year or, indeed, from one month to the next and there are now very limited mortgage options.

Self-certification mortgages were introduced to allow business owners to declare income level without actually proving the level of money earned. Unfortunately, pre-2008 this was sometimes used to obtain a level of mortgage that people who didn't own or run their own business could ill-afford to keep going.

As a result of changes to lending rules, self-certification mortgages have disappeared from the market. This is because the lender has to prove they verified your income and affordability prior to lending you the money. It doesn't mean you can't get a mortgage if you have a complicated income profile, you will just need to work closely with the lender so they are satisfied you can afford the mortgage in the long term.

Bridging loans

If you have an offer accepted on a property but can't sell yours, or are suddenly faced with a delay in selling, you may consider a bridging loan. This is a new loan while you still have your old mortgage, and it is expensive: there is usually a setting-up fee of 1–3 per cent, and the interest rate is generally 1–2.5 per cent per month.

A reputable bridging loan company would always want to be assured of a route to recoup their money, such as selling your home or re-mortgaging.

If you are in this position, you might be better off renting out your old home instead. This will allow you to move to your new property, contribution to or even cover your existing mortgage, and remove the pressure to sell fast. You could convert your existing mortgage to a **buy-to-let** arrangement by writing to your current lender asking consent to let. This is normally the least costly option before considering a re-mortgage to a buy to let.

Hidden costs

Rather like a restaurant bill where a cover charge, extra drinks, a phantom dessert and a service charge (with an extra box for 'gratuities') appear at the end to inflate the cost, mortgages can soak up more of your money than you expected. Some expensive 'extras' to watch out for include the following.

Early repayment charges

Early repayment charges (also known as redemption penalties) can apply when you repay the mortgage in full or in part. Some lenders don't charge this if you remain owing as little as £1, whereas others will charge if you pay off any amount at all, so it is important to be aware of the small print before you confirm your move and any new lending agreement.

When moving house, you effectively pay off the existing loan and take out a new one. You may, however, be charged several months' worth of mortgage payments as a penalty for redeeming earlier than stated in the agreement, unless your loan is classed as '**portable**', in which case your mortgage arrangement can be transferred to the new property.

Arrangement fee

Many lenders charge an arrangement fee for reserving

Jargon buster
Key facts about our mortgage services
An illustration showing the mortgage costs, features and terms and conditions. You should be given this for a mortgage that is recommended to you if you take advice, or one for each of the mortgages you are interested in if you don't take advice (see also pages 56-7).

funds for special deals like fixed-rate mortgages and discounted-rate mortgages. These can be a weighty expense of anything from around £400 to as high as 3 per cent of the mortgage value. Research from Moneyfacts shows that, in 2012, the average arrangement fee was £1,500, excluding deals for people with credit problems. Some lenders then suggest that you 'add' this to the mortgage, but this will cost you more in interest charges over the term of your mortgage.

Insurance fee

Some mortgage lenders charge an administration fee, which they claim is to cover the costs of a letter confirming that you have buildings insurance – if you don't take out their own. This fee can be £25 or more. If you are in a leasehold property and cannot therefore purchase your own buildings insurance, it is worth querying this charge as they may well drop it.

Higher lending charge

This is a charge you may have to pay, typically if you have a deposit of less than 10 per cent. The fee pays for insurance that protects the lender if you default on payments and they have to sell the property at a loss. It doesn't protect you in any way.

Advisers' fees

No one works for nothing, and certainly not financial advisers and mortgage brokers, who will charge a fee for advice or take commission from the lender they recommend if you sign up with them (see page 38). Fees can be up to 3 per cent of your loan, or around £75 per hour. Check this out with the mortgage broker or independent financial adviser before you commit. At the start of the meeting, the adviser should explain what level of service he or she can offer, how the adviser will be paid for it, how many lenders they search against and who regulates his or her activities (for more information, see page 50).

However, these fees can be offset by any beneficial terms the adviser negotiates on your behalf. You have a right to know what commission fee or other payment (which is declared on a document entitled **key facts about our mortgage services** – see pages 56–7) will be made to them, and can then judge for yourself if you think this is reasonable. After all, you are the one funding it.

Banking services

Your deposit and mortgage money will be transferred electronically, for which you will be charged. Fees vary from £20 to £50 and it is worth asking what they are and whether transfers can be made at the same time to avoid multiple charges.

Other products

Buying a property with a mortgage is a big financial commitment that you may choose to protect with various insurance policies. Your lender may recommend some and may insist that you have life insurance. Which policies you decide to take out will depend on your circumstances, your attitude to risk and advice you receive. You must disclose your medical history and seek independent advice.

Life insurance

This means that if you die, a lump sum equivalent to the sum insured will be paid, which should be set to the value of the mortgage – or the part of the mortgage that you are responsible for. (If you are single with no dependants, you may not need life insurance but seek advice first.) Level term assurance runs for a set period, usually the mortgage term, and is suitable if you have an interest-only mortgage as the sum assured stays the same throughout the term of the insurance. If you have a repayment mortgage, you are more likely to be advised to go for a decreasing term assurance (also known as mortgage protection cover), which guarantees to pay a reduced sum each year, matching the debt left on the loan. It tends to have lower premiums than level term assurance because the benefit reduces with time. Check regularly that your cover is sufficient to cover your outstanding debt.

Critical illness cover (CIC)

This pays the sum insured, which should be set to the value of the mortgage (or the part that you are responsible for) if you suffer a severe illness as defined in their terms and conditions. The premiums will depend on your age and general health as well as the amount of the loan. Ideally, you should find a policy that conforms to the Association of British Insurers standards which covers set illnesses. For more information, see www.abi.org.uk/Information/Consumers/. Do check what is and is not included before paying out for this type of cover.

Income protection insurance or permanent health insurance (PHI)

Permanent health insurance (PHI) pays you a regular income if you suffer from a long-term illness, which is designed to replace any loss of income from employment. Again, the premiums will depend on the same factors as critical illness cover. If you are in a full-time job, you may have this cover already – check with your employer. This insurance is permanent and can stay with you throughout your full employment.

Accident, sickness and unemployment cover

This pays out a regular income if you have an accident, are made redundant or suffer some forms of sickness. It only covers mortgage payments and is often limited to the first 12 or 24 months. This insurance is renewable annually, so beware that it can be refused in the future.

Getting the best mortgage

When you move house, you will have to reassess your mortgage: you will either have to redeem your existing one or take your current mortgage to the new property.

Whatever your decision, it makes sense at this juncture to go a step further and check whether your deal is the best on the market. Surprisingly, only half of us change lender when we move home. Lots of people also stick with their lender for buildings and contents insurance, mortgage protection and life cover, which is convenient but can be expensive versus other companies. It pays to shop around.

Start by familiarising yourself with the types of mortgages on offer (as explained in this book on pages 42–4). Start by talking to your existing lender if you have one to see what they can offer. Also consult a mortgage broker or independent financial adviser or someone else that you trust or has previously helped a friend or relative, and then compare and query the advice.

Mortgage lenders and intermediaries

Under mortgage regulations, lenders and intermediaries must either be authorised by the Financial Services Authority (or Financial Conduct Authority (FCA) from 2013) or be an appointed representative of an authorised firm. Lenders and intermediaries offer two levels of service that you will be asked to choose from.

- **Advised service:** you will receive a recommendation on which of the mortgages that they can provide is most suitable for you. If the mortgage turns out to be the wrong one for you, you can complain to the firm and you claim compensation for any loss. Unless you are very confident about choosing a mortgage yourself, it makes sense to opt for the advised service.
- **Non-advised service:** you'll receive information only and will be responsible for making your own choice. The lender will

> **'It pays to shop around for a mortgage but take plenty of advice, too, such as from a mortgage broker or IFA.'**

ask you pre-scripted questions to narrow down the mortgages on which they give you information. This level of service offers much less protection.

Services and costs disclosure document

When you first contact a firm, you should be given a document entitled 'Key facts about our mortgage services' (this is also known as a services and costs disclosure document – SCDD). It will set out whether the adviser is going to give you advice and a recommendation or just information, whether you will pay a fee for the service and whose mortgages it offers. For example, lenders, such as banks and building societies, can usually only recommend mortgages from their own range, whereas a broker may search the whole market or be linked to a selection of lenders.

The right mortgage

To make the choice of mortgage that is right for you, you need to ask the right questions and be sure that you understand the answers (see overleaf and pages 54–5). A good financial adviser, whether an independent person or a representative of a lender, should be able to explain the pros and

The cost of advice

If you ask an individual or company to search the market for mortgages for you, such as a broker, you may be charged as much as 2 or 3 per cent of the mortgage. So on a £100,000 loan, you could pay up to £3,000 for the advice. They may otherwise take commission from the lender.

From January 2013, independent financial advisers may charge for their advice rather than taking commission for financial advice. This advice is likely to cost around £75 an hour plus VAT or up to 3 per cent of the mortgage.

Make sure you are clear about whether you are being given advice on all mortgages available or a limited number and how much this advice will cost you.

cons of your various options and justify the advice that is given. If the adviser proves unable to do this to your satisfaction, you should take your custom elsewhere.

An adviser should start discussions with you with a financial audit similar in approach to that on pages 24–35. They will also ask you about your attitude to risk and your opinion on interest rates as this has a bearing on the product they will suggest.

'Always read the 'Key facts' document.'

To find an independent financial adviser, go to **www.fsa.gov.uk** (FCA from 2013, see page 25) , **www.unbiased.co.uk** and **www.find.co.uk**. Check on **www.fsa. gov.uk/fsaregister** to see if your adviser is authorised to offer advice. See also **www.whichmortgageadvisers.co.uk** for impartial advice on mortgages.

Key questions to ask your adviser

Here is a checklist of key questions that will help you make your decision as to which adviser to give your mortgage business to. Your adviser should give you all this information when you contact them as a document entitled 'Key facts about our mortgage services'.

'Are you authorised to give mortgage advice?'

Advisers must either be directly authorised as an individual by the FSA (FCA from 2013, see page 25) or represent an FSA authorised firm. You can check if they are covered by the regulations on www.moneyadviceservice.org.uk. They should also have passed the Certificate in Mortgage Advice and Practice (CMAP) or Financial Planning Certificate (FPC) with a Mortgage Advice Qualification (MAQ).

'How much of the mortgage market do you have access to?'

Lenders usually only offer mortgages from their own mortgage range. Some IFAs and mortgage brokers only offer mortgages from their preferred lenders, which could restrict the choice of products they make available to you.

'What level of service do you provide?'

They may make a recommendation after they have assessed your needs or provide information only and leave you to choose which mortgage to go for. Only if you buy with advice can you complain to the firm and expect compensation if the mortgage turns out to be unsuitable.

'How will you charge me for advice?'

Intermediaries will either charge you a fee or be paid commission by the lender. They must tell you which of these applies and how much they expect to earn from your transaction. In effect, you are paying for their time and expertise (see page 51).

Key questions about your mortgage

Make sure your adviser covers the following points to ensure you get as much information about the mortgages on offer as possible. Much of this information should be covered in the key facts illustration your adviser will give you.

'What types of mortgage are available, what are their advantages and disadvantages and how would they suit me?'

The advice should include references to the types of mortgage referred to on pages 42–3.

'What different ways can I repay my mortgage and what are their pros and cons?'

You should be told about repayment and interest-only mortgages including the various ways of repaying the loan sum for the latter.

'What are the risks?'

Your adviser should explain the difference in risk between repayment and interest-only mortgages. You should also be told about the risks of variable rate mortgages and the risk of your income falling.

'What is the interest rate and how does it compare with the Bank of England base rate?'

The adviser should explain what the rate is, how long it applies for and if it is variable or fixed. If there is an initial rate, the adviser should also tell you what it will change to and when.

Key questions about your mortgage

continued

'Can I afford this mortgage?'

If you're getting advice, your adviser has a duty to take reasonable steps to ensure you can afford the mortgage he or she recommends. Even if you don't get advice, the adviser should check that you can afford the repayments now and in the future.

'How much are the monthly payments? What would they be if the variable rate rises by 1, 3 or 5 percentage points?'

This information will help you decide if you are able to face the risk of higher payments. You should also be told the effect of any change of rate after the initial period.

'How much will I pay in total, including any fees?'

To compare mortgages, you need to know the full cost, including any fees you'll pay. Check whether you would have to pay any of the fees if the house purchase falls through. If fees are added to the mortgage, rather than paying them upfront, you will pay interest on them for the whole term, so check out how much you would be paying in interest on these fees and make a decision as to whether you would be better off paying them separately if you can.

'What might change the interest rate and what notice will I receive?'

If you opt for a rate that is not fixed, it is useful to know how often your interest rates will be reviewed and whether any relationship to the Bank of England base rate might change your payments.

'What if I repay my mortgage early?'

Early repayment charges may apply if you repay the mortgage in the early years. Make sure you understand how much you would have to pay.

'Would I be charged if I made extra payments?'

Early repayment charges can be charged if you pay off any monies over and above your regular monthly mortgage payments (see page 47). Alternatively, you may be able to pay off a certain amount extra each month or year.

'What if my circumstances change?'

Your adviser will have full knowledge of how any changes in your circumstances may affect your ability to pay your mortgage or associated protection policies, and should indicate how flexible the lender can be.

'Can I take the mortgage with me if I move?'

You should be able to do so but there may be conditions attached. Your mortgage lender or financial adviser should tell you of any restrictions.

'What if I miss or am late with a payment?'

Lenders must have a written policy on this issue and make clear any charges for falling into arrears. Check what these are before you agree to the mortgage.

'How long will it take to process my application?'

This could be really important if you've already had an offer accepted on a property. Most lenders will give you a Mortgage Agreement in Principle (MAP) within minutes (see page 40) but it can then take from a few weeks to six weeks for a mortgage lender to confirm their offer.

What you need when arranging a mortgage

A mortgage is a loan of a massive amount of money so obviously the lender will need to check who you are and your financial details. When you go to a mortgage interview you will need:

- **Proof of identity,** such as a driving licence, utility bill or passport.
- **Proof of income** – three recent payslips or your latest P60. Bringing a letter from your employer confirming your earnings will save time as the lender will ask for this.
- **Your bank account** details.
- **Your current mortgage** account number and amount outstanding.
- **Any other addresses** you have lived at, if you haven't lived in your own property for three years or more.
- **Details of existing insurance policies** such as life insurance and income protection.

It would also be useful if you have:

- **Evidence** of your expenditure (such as the table on page 27). This will show that you are serious about buying and have thought about what you can realistically afford.
- **Proof** of where you live (such as two recent utility bills).
- **Information** about the property you are selling.
- **Details of the property** you would like to buy, assuming you actually know this.

Key facts illustrations (KFI)

Once you have decided on which mortgage you want or your adviser has recommended one to you, your adviser will then provide a summary of the mortgage. Known as the key facts illustration, it provides details of the features, terms and conditions of the mortgage in a standardised format. It should enable you to compare different lenders' products on the same basis. It is personalised to you and the amount that you want to borrow. Among other things, the KFI will tell you:

- The overall cost of the mortgage.
- The cost of your regular payments.
- The initial interest rate and what it will rise to after any special deal ends.
- Whether there are any penalties for overpaying.
- What happens if you repay the mortgage early or move house.

Surf and save

It is well worth checking out mortgage deals on the internet, even if it is only to be reassured that you have got a reasonable deal. The best thing to do is to go to a mortgage comparison site such as the ones on www.whichmortgageadvisers.co.uk/mortgage-deals/ or www.moneynet.co.uk/mortgages.

- Whether there are any conditional products that you must buy, such as insurance.
- If it's a variable rate mortgage, it will also include an illustration of the amount by which your regular payments would increase if the base rate were to rise by 1 per cent.

'Use the hints and tips on this page and overleaf to make sure that you steer clear of all bad advice that may still be out there, despite the best efforts of the FSA.'

How to avoid getting bad advice

Following the regulation of advice and sale of products by the FSA (FCA from 2013, see page 25), getting the right information about mortgages and related financial products should be easier and more professional. Here are some hints and tips to make sure that you steer clear of all bad advice that may still be out there!

- **Work out your monthly budget** so that you know how much you can afford to pay, allowing for changes in interest rates (see page 36).
- **Be clear about your attitude to risk:** do you mind the prospect of costs going up as well as down, or prefer the reassurance of knowing exactly what you'll be paying each month?
- **Go to an independent mortgage adviser** unless you are very confident that you know exactly what you want. They can recommend most mortgages and services, rather than tied advisers, who only sell their own company's loans, or advisers who only offer a selection of lenders

and their products. To find an independent mortgage adviser, see the box at the foot of page 51.

- **If you get advice from a mortgage lender,** you will have to compare the cost of rival mortgages yourself, which can be time-consuming and confusing as you will not always be comparing like with like. Independent financial advisers and brokers should do this for you.
- **Choose the 'advised' level of service,** rather than the 'information-only' level (see page 50), which puts all the responsibility for the final choice onto you. Check this on the services and costs disclosure document – SCDD (see page 51), which should be produced right at the start of the meeting.
- **Ask questions** about anything you do not understand (it is the adviser's job to make it clear) and compare costs by monthly payment and total cost over the time you expect to keep the mortgage loan for.

- **Get costings** on different mortgage terms such as 15, 25 and 30 years. Longer loans may mean lower monthly payments but a higher repayment to the lender over the term of the mortgage.
- **Tell your adviser** if you think you'll be able to make overpayments or pay the loan off early: it will affect the choice of mortgage deal.
- **Be clear** about what is being recommended, its cost implications, the fees and charges involved. Study the KFI and check you understand it or ask your adviser if you have any more questions.
- **Ask your adviser** why he or she is recommending this deal and make sure that you are given a satisfactory rationale that is appropriate for your circumstances. You should receive confirmation in the post detailing the mortgage deal

BE CAREFUL!
If you think you have ever geen advised badly, you may have grounds for a mis-selling complaint.

and reasons for the adviser's recommendation, which is normally referred to as a 'suitability letter'.

- **Think about your finances** and decide how important it would be to have a flexible mortgage where you can overpay or take a holiday (see pages 45–6), or whether you don't mind payments varying, or if your priority is to keep costs down in the short-term when you may be more strapped for cash.

Badly advised?

If you think you were badly advised, go to the firm who advised you (they will be named in the Services and Costs Disclosure Document) and ask for a copy of their complaints procedure. Follow the procedure, but if the issue is not resolved to your satisfaction, go to the Financial Ombudsman Service (FOS). They will investigate your complaint and make a binding adjudication, which is only binding on the lender, not on you. If you don't accept this adjudication, your only recourse is then to go to court. Contact the FOS via www.financialombudsman.org.uk or on 0845 080 1800.

'Be clear about your attitude to risk: do you mind the propspect of costs going up as well as down, or prefer the reassurance of knowing exactly what you'll be paying each month?'

Mortgage problems

It is possible that something happens when you are buying or have bought your home that means you either can't get a mortgage, or once you have one, you can't afford to pay it.

This section helps to explain why you might be rejected for a mortgage, what you can do about it and then looks at what to do if you get into trouble.

Getting a mortgage

There are a number of reasons why it can be difficult to get a mortgage. These are the main ones.

No deposit

One of the effects of falling property prices is that 100 per cent mortgages were withdrawn due to the risk of the lender not getting their money back if the mortgagee defaulted on the payments and the lender had to repossess the property.

There are few alternatives, but you can talk to new build companies who may offer to pay the deposit on their property for you as part of an incentive to purchase. But check the lender will agree to this. The only other way is to ask friends and family to help raise the deposit, which could be up to 25 per cent, and in return you could offer them a percentage share in the property.

Self-employed

The self-employed or those with irregular incomes cannot always provide the financial information to reassure a lender that they are safe to lend to. Again, some are happy to lend in these circumstances (see page 32).

Retiring soon

Many people opt to downsize their home when they no longer need lots of space and spare rooms. If you still need a mortgage when downsizing and nearing retirement, you may be restricted on the loan period or the amount they will lend you.

Poor credit record

When you apply for a mortgage, the lender is likely to run checks with credit reference agencies. They are basically looking to find out what your credit history is like, in other words, if you have a history of bad debts or property repossessions. You can check the information held on you with the main agencies via www.creditexpert.co.uk, www.equifax.co.uk and www.callcredit.co.uk. This is well worth doing as the information they hold can be inaccurate or out of date (see page 32). The charge for a report from a CRA is £2 if sent by post. You can obtain reports online but charges may vary. A specialist broker or lender may still be able to help to get you a mortgage, although you are likely to be charged higher interest rates. If you maintain regular payments, you may be able to re-negotiate more favourable terms after three years.

BE CAREFUL!

If a lender rejects your application, find out why and then talk to an experienced independent mortgage adviser, if you haven't already. However, remember you will have to inform them that a previous application has been refused. Double-check that you haven't been turned down due to credit reference issues or other information on your paperwork that may not be accurate (see page 32).

Affordable home ownership

If you are on a low income, a first-time buyer or are an existing social rented tenant, you may be able to access a scheme that helps you onto the housing ladder. These schemes might be run by a local council, housing association, or via a private developer. Schemes for first-time buyers are on pages 139–42. You will need to check if you are eligible, but schemes for social rented tenants include:

■ **The Right to Buy (RTB) scheme** in which, under certain circumstances, social rented tenants can purchase the property they rent from a local authority and, if eligible, may gain a discount on the purchase.

■ **The Right to Acquire (RTA) scheme** allows some social rented tenants to purchase the property they rent from a housing association. Discounts on the purchase range from £9,000 to £16,000.

■ **Social HomeBuy** allows some other eligible social rented tenants (who are not eligible for RTB or RTA) to purchase part or all of their housing association or council home via shared ownership. You can buy from 25 per cent of the property and pay rent on the rest.

If you are a social tenant wishing to purchase a property under any of these schemes, contact your landlord for more information.

For an application form for Right to Buy if you are a social rented tenant go to **www.homesandcommunities.co.uk** or **www.homebuy.co.uk**. See also pages 139–42, which explain what options are available to you.

Problems with the property

The lender may be reluctant to loan on properties in a poor state of repair, short leases, unusual houses or flats (such as being located over a shop), or houses made of unusual materials, even thatched properties. There are, however, lenders who are willing to lend on 'non-standard' properties. For properties in a poor state of repair or non-standard properties, find an IFA or mortgage broker who knows which lenders to turn to.

If you can't afford to pay your mortgage

There are many reasons why people can hit difficulties in meeting their monthly mortgage payment, such as long-term illness, relationship breakdown or unemployment.

If you are having trouble meeting mortgage payments, the first course of action should be to tell your lender. It is in their interest to help you out rather than instigate an expensive and time-consuming repossession on your property.

Don't forget that if you don't sort out the issues and payments with your lender, you wouldn't just lose your home, but it would also be very difficult for you to get any more loans or a mortgage again.

It may be that you can get help with your mortgage payments. Remember that your lender will want to help you solve the problem now, rather than allow things to get worse. If you aren't getting much help from a local office, then contact their head office. Check, too, to see if you have got any cover, such as accident, sickness and unemployment, critical illness cover or income protection (see page 49) that may pay out for you.

Arrangements that a mortgage lender may offer you in order to help you during difficulties making mortgage payments include the various possibilities that are outlined in full below and overleaf.

Fair enough?

Lenders are currently regulated by the FSA (FCA from 2013, see page 25), whose rules state they must 'deal fairly with any customer who is in arrears'. They must have a written policy on arrears, set up a feasible payment plan for you, and update you regularly on your arrears without applying pressure with excessive telephone calls or letters. However, you must make every effort to keep up with the new payment plan.

Mortgage rescue schemes

At the time of going to print there were various schemes to help with mortgage payments, but these are likely to change over time, so check with your lender and secure free help from organisations such as the National Debtline and visit www.direct.gov.uk.

First, most lenders have signed up to offer Homeowners Mortgage Support schemes to help you stay in your home as opposed to being repossessed, especially if you are struggling to make payments due to a temporary drop in income, for example due to illness or job loss.

Check if your lender has signed up to this scheme and, if not, what other help they can give you. If you are really struggling to pay your mortgage and are highly likely to be repossessed and cannot secure help from your lender, contact your local authority housing department.

They may be able to help organise a local housing association that could offer a low interest loan against your property to reduce your monthly repayments. In some cases, they may even buy the majority of your home and you can stay in the property and pay rent as their tenant.

Paying interest only

Your lender may accept a monthly payment covering only the interest on your mortgage for a short period of time, which may help you sort out your finances and return to paying a repayment mortgage or continuing to pay your savings plan if you have an interest-only mortgage.

Extend the mortgage term

The standard term for a mortgage is 25 years but lenders may consider increasing this by five or ten years. It may also be that you only have 15 or 20 years left on your current mortgage, so it would be easier to extend the payment to 25 years. This would bring down the cost of your monthly payments, but don't forget that in the long term you would be paying more back because of the additional interest charges over the extra term.

Payment agreement

If the amount that you can't afford to pay is only temporary, you can offer an extra monthly payment in the future to clear the arrears. This could be over a few months or a few years, depending what term is feasible for you and what the lender will accept. Even if you can't agree an amount with your lender in the short term, pay what you can, explaining in writing what you are doing and why. If the value of your home is greater than the outstanding loan on your mortgage, let the lender know as you may be able to re-mortgage and pay back the arrears over the lifetime of the mortgage.

The mortgage is then re-negotiated and the arrears added to the total loan, spreading the cost over the remaining years of the term. This would increase your monthly mortgage payments, but help spread the cost of the arrears over a longer period of time so you don't have to find a large lump sum to pay.

 If you have payment problems, contact National Debtline on **www.nationaldebtline.co.uk** and/or go to **www.clsdirect. org.uk**, **www.citizensadvice.org.uk**, **www.cccs.co.uk** and **www.shelter.org.uk**.

If you can't cover the mortgage in any way

You may decide or be advised that you can't cover the mortgage on any terms. Some people just hand in the keys, but this doesn't mean you don't owe the lender money any more. In fact, you will still be charged the monthly instalments on the mortgage. Any debts you accrue from this will be added with interest to what you owe. Then, when the house is sold, the lenders' legal fees, the estate agent's fees and any court costs that are incurred when trying to recover monies from you will be added to the monies owed.

Another alternative is to sell your property to cover your debts, repay the mortgage lender and move to a cheaper, smaller home, or look at renting from a housing association if you are eligible. It may also be possible to rent out the home for a while – if this means you can pay the bills, then it has to be worth having a go. You may even be able to move in with friends or relatives for a while.

If you do sell your property and still owe money to the lender, make sure you come to an arrangement where you can continue to afford to pay off the monies.

The pitfalls of rushing into an 'emergency sale'

Quick sale

This is where someone offers to buy your property quickly for cash so you can avoid being repossessed. Be aware that they may offer a price much lower than the property is worth. They will try to obtain it for about 80 per cent or less of its real market value – even in a difficult market. First, talk to local estate agents and get a valuation survey on your property so that you have a good idea of the true value. Many buyers would be happy to buy at a 10 per cent discount so explore other opportunities first.

Sale and leaseback

This is where a company/buyer will offer to buy your property at a discount (20 per cent or more off the true property value) and then let the home back to you. Although the FSA (FCA from 2013, see page 25) regulated companies offering these services in 2010, most have now stopped doing any business, so this is not an option to consider. You could end up selling your home for a lot less than it's worth, or an unscrupulous buyer may suggest you can continue renting but then throw you out after a year! A better idea is to see if you are eligible for a mortgage rescue scheme or to sell the property and rent another one instead.

Mortgage problems

Assets, advisers and affordability

Insuring your home

Insurance is a vital part of protecting your home and belongings. There are two kinds of insurance that you will need to look into: buildings and contents insurance.

Buildings insurance covers the cost of rebuilding your home if it is damaged. You won't be able to exchange on a property until this is organised.

Contents insurance covers your possessions. It is not compulsory and about a quarter of UK households don't have it. They are taking a big risk.

Many mortgage lenders also sell contents and buildings insurance, but it is always worth shopping around to get the best deal and some companies can offer much better rates than your incumbent lender. There are also some circumstances that may require specialist insurance – for example, if you work from home and need to cover all of your business equipment, or if you have a thatched cottage.

Buildings insurance

The sum insured must be enough to pay for the cost of rebuilding your home if it is severely damaged by fire, storms, flooding or other catastrophes. This is usually lower than the value of your property because it only covers the bricks and mortar and labour to rebuild your property, not the cost of the land.

As a rough guide, the cost of rebuilding a home is approximately 75 per cent of its value, but the insurance company will verify this for you. If you want guidance on the figure, a surveyor should be able to help and you can use online calculators too (see www.abi.org. uk). Insurers will need to know various details about the property, including the following:

- **What year** it was built.
- **Type of construction,** such as brick and tile construction, or nineteenth-century stone, or timber framed houses.
- **Postcode** of the property to check for flooding or other environmental risks (see pages 147–9).
- **How many bedrooms**/rooms the property has.

At risk of flood?

Two million homes in England and Wales are at risk of flooding, 40 per cent of these are classified as a high risk at a time when our climate is

Administration fee

Check if your mortgage lender is going to charge you an administration fee for buying another company's buildings insurance policy and make sure that this is less than the saving you make and/or that the policy you choose covers you for more circumstances than the lender's. If you have no choice of building insurance (for example, you are buying a leasehold/commonhold property), then ask the lender or your IFA if this charge can be withdrawn.

changing. Insurers will assess your risk of flooding from your postcode and other information they have. However, different insurers can consider different postcodes as high or low risk, depending on the information they have. For example, if you live near a river but are on a hill, your risk of flooding is a lot less than someone in the same postcode at the bottom of the hill. Your insurer may not take this into account though as some insurers use full postcodes, some don't. Depending on the insurer, you may get a cheaper or more expensive quote. Many companies are refusing to insure new customers who have made a flooding claim

in the past. However, all insurance companies who are members of the Association of British Insurers have signed up to a statement of principles, which lays out how the insurance companies could possibly help residential properties that are on a floodplain.

What the insurance covers

Buildings insurance covers the reconstruction of your home, including fixtures and fittings, if it is destroyed or damaged by anything out of your control such as:

- Subsidence.
- Storm and flood damage.
- Burst pipes and other water leaks.
- Fire, smoke and explosions (excluding acts of war or terrorism).
- Vandalism or third-party damage.

Cover usually includes the basic structure plus all windows, the roof, kitchen and bathroom, floors, electrical wiring and plumbing. External constructions, such as a conservatory, shed, garage or greenhouse, are also generally covered. Do not assume every policy covers every possibility. As always, read the small print and if you are not clear on a point, ask the insurer or your broker.

Any flood defence measures in your area may help you get a better deal with an insurance company. These sites help identify if the property is at risk from flooding: **www.environment-agency.gov.uk/homeandleisure** and **www.homecheck.co.uk**.

Consider the level of cover that you need. Never under insure your property, but also don't pay more than you have to by over-insuring. An unlimited policy may be worth looking at if you have a lot of things that have a high value, which may nevertheless need to be insured separately.

In your research it is worth checking these points:

- ■ **Do you have the right level** of cover? Make sure everything is taken into account, such as any previous claims or subsidence problems.
- ■ **Do they have a 24-hour** helpline for claims?
- ■ **What would the excess be** and how much less would your insurance cost if you paid a higher excess? (Don't pay monthly as you will pay more – as much as 10–30 per cent.)

> 'Buildings insurance allows for reconstruction of your home, including fixtures and fittings, if it is destroyed or damaged by anything out of your control.'

BE CAREFUL!

If the property you are buying is leasehold, as is the case with most flats, check that the freeholder or managing agent has taken out a buildings insurance policy and if you are liable for part of the cost of this policy. You should ask for a copy of the policy so you can check if you need to take out further insurance, and so that you can supply its detail to your conveyancer and lender before exchanging contracts.

- ■ **Would the insurer pay** to house you while your property is being rebuilt or repaired, and what kind of accommodation would it fund and how long for?
- ■ **Would you receive** any interim payments during this period or would they pay costs direct to the supplier?
- ■ **Would you have some input** in the way the house is rebuilt?
- ■ **Would the policy cover** the cost of clearing away any debris and rubble?
- ■ **Are architects** and surveyors or other fees included?
- ■ **How long** does it usually take to assess and settle a claim? The company should be able to give you a guideline.

Further information on buildings insurance, including rebuilding costs, is available from the Association of British Insurers (**www.abi.org.uk**) and from the Building Cost Information Service (BCIS) (**www.bcis.co.uk**) as well as **www.which.co.uk/homeinsurance**.

Contents insurance

This provides protection for your possessions inside the home if they are damaged, destroyed or stolen. It can also cover things outside the house, if you pay extra and as long as they aren't taken off the property altogether. It should include just about everything you would take with you if you moved home – furniture and furnishings, household goods, kitchen equipment, televisions, DVD and video players, computer and audio equipment, clothing, personal effects, and valuables – up to stated limits.

When taking out a policy you will be asked about:

- **Whether you are leaving** the property unoccupied during the day.
- **If you are out of the country** for long periods (more than a month or two).
- **What security devices** are fitted, such as an alarm.
- **Your employment.**
- **Past house insurance** claims.
- **If you have a criminal** record.
- **Your postcode,** which insurers use to calculate the level of risk and which can significantly influence the premium.
- **Any other factor** that influences the security or risk of damage to your items, such as if you are self-employed and regularly take a laptop or other expensive equipment away with you.

Level of cover

Most policies set a limit on the overall amount you can claim, known as the **sum insured**. Some insurers stick to a set sum insured (usually between a maximum of £50,000 and £100,000), others are happy to customise the policy to your needs, while some give **unlimited cover**.

Working out the value of your possessions is an essential process, although you don't have to go into so much detail if your policy is **bedroom rated** (see definition overleaf). Note down everything in each room and estimate what it is worth. Keep receipts for valuable items as a record and even take photographs. It is advisable to get an expert valuation on any unusual or expensive valuables, art or antiques, so that you know you have it insured for the right amount. It is important to review your sum insured regularly, at least once a year, to allow for the cost of any items you purchase.

Moving?

If you are selling your house, ensure you keep the insurance cover in place until you have completed. Then you can cancel it and possibly claim a refund on any monies outstanding if you have not made a claim that year. Alternatively, you could, of course, transfer the policy to your new home. To save time you can do this at time of exchange.

It is generally agreed in the insurance industry that most people undervalue their possessions. If this is proved to be the case, your insurer will only pay out the amount you insured with them or less, rather than the true item value. So if you insure for £50K and the property is worth £100K and you claim for £50K, you will only get 50 per cent of this, which equals £25K. Make sure your policy is updated on an annual basis.

Replacement as new versus indemnity cover

Most companies only insure new for old, although some offer indemnity cover as well.

Replacement as new (also known as new for old)

This pays the full cost of repairing or replacing damaged or lost articles with brand new ones. Most policies exclude clothing and household linen.

> **'It is a wise precaution to get an expert valuation on any unusual valuables.'**

Jargon buster

Accidental damage Extra cover to insure against accidental damage to your possessions although a standard policy will include some accidental cover.

All-risk basis Additional cover for your possessions if you are away from home. Also known as personal possessions cover.

Bedroom-rated policy Some contents insurance policies allow you to opt for insurance based on the number of bedrooms your property has. If you use a bedroom for another purpose – as an office, say – it still counts as a bedroom for insurance. Some offer unlimited cover, while others still require you to value your possessions.

Sum insured The amount for which you have insured your property or items. For example, it might be £30,000 for contents or £175,000 for rebuilding cost. This is the 'sum' you have 'insured' and are paying annually or monthly for. If something goes wrong, it is the most the insurer will pay out.

Unlimited cover Where there is no upper value, which is worth considering if you have many high-value possessions, although remember that you will have to specify individually any high-value items.

The website of the Association of British Insurers (**www.abi.org.uk**) has a free spreadsheet you can download to help you calculate how much your contents are worth. Go to the consumer section within the 'information zone' on their website.

High-value items

If you have some high-value items you have several options:

- Ensure they are specifically listed in the policy with their value, and photograph them.
- Insure them separately (for example, some insurers specialise in musical instrument or cycle cover) or add them to your policy for a charge.
- Break down the item into component parts of lower value (such as the separate parts of a hi-fi system, or the lenses, main body and peripherals of a camera).

Sometimes age limits also apply.

Indemnity cover

This makes a deduction in the value to allow for wear and tear and depreciation, so premiums will be cheaper – but you'll only get the second-hand value of your possessions. Because of this you may be asked, and need to prove the year, in which certain items were acquired.

Your responsibilities

You are expected to keep the insured possessions in a good state of repair and take all reasonable steps to prevent loss or damage occurring to them. Most policies will cover loss or damage to your possessions while in your home by:

- Fire, explosion, lightning or earthquake
- Subsidence, heave or landslide
- Storm and flood
- Theft or attempted theft
- Escape of water from tanks or pipes
- Falling trees or branches
- Breakage or collapse of television, radio signal or satellite apparatus
- Riot, civil commotion, strikes, labour or political disturbances
- Impact by aircraft, other aerial devices, any vehicle or animal
- Escape of oil from heating systems.

Policies can be extended to cover **accidental damage** to or loss of items that you may take out of your home. This can cover such items as clothing, jewellery, cameras and sports equipment (which you might also decide to insure on an all-risk basis, so they are covered away from your home). Further cover can be arranged to insure personal money and credit cards, cycles and legal expenses. If you extend a policy, your premium may go up, so it is worth shopping around to see if you can get a better deal. You will also pay a higher premium if you opt for cover for possessions outside of the home.

'**Ensure high-value items are specifically listed and take a photo of them. This is essential if you use a removal's packing service.**'

Moving house?

Remember to notify your current contents insurers of the date of your move. However, if the move is going to take more than a day to be completed, get them to hold the cover on both addresses.

Check also if the policy covers your possessions during the move, as this is a time when things can be easily damaged. If it doesn't cover them, ask your removal company if they have insurance that will cover your possessions during the move (see page 169).

Other things that you need to consider are:

- **Whether the policy covers** accidental damage (there is usually an extra charge for this).
- **Are valuables insured** in transit and while you are on holiday?
- **If the policy covers** any lost or stolen cash and if there is a limit on the amount.
- **See also the checklist** on buildings insurance (pages 65–6).

How much you will pay

Premiums on buildings and contents policies change every year, so you can save money by shopping around annually. The buildings element is usually index-linked to the retail price index so a series of natural disasters can increase the price of your policy, as can several years of high claim levels. The number of years that you have not made a claim for also makes a difference to your

You may be required to pay the first part of a claim yourself (from £50 to £500 or so) – this is called the 'excess'. Excesses are applied to a range of claims and you can set the excess to be higher or lower, which may decrease or increase the monthly or annual premium. The level of discount will increase with the size of excess you choose: the higher the excess, the lower your premium. Also note that subsidence excess can be much higher – ranging from £1,000 to £2,000.

Your policy will exclude certain risks or possessions. Common exclusions are theft if you have let or sub-let your house (or part of it), unless there is forced entry, or loss or damage arising if you leave your house unoccupied for long periods (typically, more than 30 days).

Shop around

In a past edition of the Which? magazine, a survey of 2,104 Which? members reported that 26 per cent bought their home insurance from their mortgage lender, yet by shopping around they could have saved at least £30 a year on their bill. (Figures quoted are for a three-bedroom house in a 'low-risk postcode'.) For information on insurance Best Buys visit www.which. co.uk/homeinsurance.

premium. The more years you haven't claimed for the better, as you can get a no claims discount up to a maximum percentage. You can also keep your costs as low as possible by:

- **Shopping around** for the best deal and insurance package to suit your specific needs.
- **Buying buildings and contents insurance** as a package, which reduces administration overheads and prevents a dispute between two insurers about who should pay a claim.
- **Being careful** not to over or under insure the building or contents.
- **Avoiding paying** for cover you don't need. For example, if you haven't got a garage, ensure you aren't paying for one.
- **Agree to pay an excess,** such as the first £200 of any claim (the standard excess is £50). Paying a larger excess can reduce premiums.
- **Fit good locks** to doors and especially windows and other entry points to a property. Ask if your insurer stipulates certain kinds or standard of locks, or gives a discount if they are in place. The Association of British Insurers (www.abi.org. uk) recommends that outside doors have a five-lever mortice deadlock with a steel striking plate, which conforms to BS3621.

- **Join a neighbourhood watch scheme.** This can earn a discount of up to 15 per cent.
- **If at all possible,** pay the premium straightaway. Opting for monthly payments can incur higher charges over the year – sometimes adding up to 30 per cent on to the premium.

> '**Shop around annually for buildings and contents policies as premiums change. Consider buying them as a package as this reduces administration overheads.**'

Where to go

Many companies in this field exploit the easy-going consumer who does not research the market. Insurance is often an add-on to other discussions about, say, mortgages, and you may be reluctant to hold up proceedings by shopping around at this stage. This is a mistake. Bank or lender insurance premiums can be significantly higher than those of the other 9,000 brokers operating in

For websites that offer you insurance comparisons, check out the following website addresses: **www.confused.com**, **www.lowermybills.co.uk** and **www.1stquote.co.uk**.

a highly competitive market. Do not rely on your mortgage provider to give you the best deal. So make sure you shop around!

> 'In your research for insurance it is important to compare quotes that are like with like so that you are looking at the whole deal and not just the price.'

BE CAREFUL!
Once you have purchased your insurance, you will be sent a copy of the policy. While it is tempting to file it away, read it first to check the accuracy of the details and ensure it covers everything agreed. Keep the policy where you can retrieve it easily in case of an urgent claim.

How to compare insurance quotes

In your research for insurance it is important that you try to compare quotes that are like with like so that you are looking at the whole deal and not just the price. If you have the time, consider doing all the research online, although you should remember that the internet is not comprehensive. Most insurers have their own websites, but, of course, these only cover their own policies. A broker will be able to choose from a wider selection, or there are many insurance comparison sites that search more widely than anyone else (for some examples, see box, below).

Bear in mind that no one site is comprehensive and it can be difficult to know if you are comparing like with like: you'll need to check policy details with the provider when you are close to making your choice.

Websites with detailed information on all the subjects covered in this section are the Financial Ombudsman Service (**www.financialombudsman.org.uk**), the Financial Services Authority (**www.fsa.gov.uk**) (FCA from 2013, see page 25), and **www.which.co.uk/homeinsurance**.

Valuing a property

3

A common mistake is to try to buy or sell property without understanding the market. In this crucial, life-changing process, it is vital that you have some understanding of the national conditions, and the vagaries of your local market. Only then can you compare like with like and make informed decisions about what a home is worth.

Understanding the market

If we were to believe all the press reports and media spin about property prices, we could quite easily think that there is only one property market.

If the press says property prices have risen by 10 per cent, then all property prices have risen by 10 per cent. The problem with this is that the next week another report might say that property prices have stayed the same, or even fallen. As a result, it is difficult to understand what is happening to property prices in the 'market' - this is because there isn't just 'one' property market. Property prices are dependent on many factors. Prices across the country tend to vary according to the general state of the economy and how confident people are about their job prospects, and therefore their attitude to buying and selling a home. They also depend on how many properties are on the market and how many people want to buy. However, the key point in understanding property prices is that they are mostly influenced by local factors, not national ones.

Although property prices do go up or down across the country as a whole, the 'buying and selling property market' covers between 1.2 and 1.5 million homes per year, although since 2008, this figure has fallen well below 1 million. Some of these properties might be brand new flats in one area, others might be old character properties. Some local economies might be expanding, others might be suffering from loss of a major employer. Depending on the number of buyers and sellers of flats or old properties, then prices in each of these areas could be going up or down – and at the same time.

The other important factor is that the same property can vary in price from one month to the next. This all depends on how many buyers there are and how many other similar properties there are for sale in the area.

To understand the market even more, it is important to compare property prices - see pages 83-8. If you are buying a property, see also pages 124-32 for information on the different types.

Why prices can vary

Imagine the scenario that you put your three-bedroomed house with a garage and garden up for sale. At the time you put your property on the market, there are few other similar properties available and lots of people are looking to buy one like yours. As a result, your estate agent puts it on the market at what they believe is a maximum price of £185,000. You get two or three offers and maybe there is even a bidding war and you end up getting £187,000 for your property.

Two months later your neighbour – whose property is the same as yours and decorated to the same standard – puts their property on the market and, seeing your price, the estate agent suggests a price of £190,000, hoping to get £187,000. However, by now, others in your locality have put their properties up for sale and there is some competition. One of the sellers needs to move urgently so their home is priced at £180,000 for a 'quick sale'. Suddenly the price for the neighbour's property looks high, and there is more choice, so to sell the property even a few months after you have, they may have to accept several thousand pounds less than you did.

Online sold property prices

One facility that is very useful are 'sold property prices' online. These allow you to find out what prices other homes in the street you are buying on have sold for recently and back as far as 1999. Not all sites have every sold property price, so it is worth having a look at different ones including: www.nethouseprices. com; www.mouseprice.com and www.rightmove.co.uk. Most of the property-finding portals also have sold price data feeds.

Using these feeds, some sites such as www.zoopla.co.uk provide free estimates for what they think a property is worth. Others, such as www.propertycheck.co.uk, provide estimated valuations but you have to pay for these. Zoopla base their estimates on a mix of past and current data that is regularly updated. As a result, they can be

---

Jargon buster

Asking price Price a seller hopes to achieve.
Bidding war When more than one party is interested in buying a property and so they bid up the price.
Property price survey Research that shows the prices of properties across the country.
Selling price Price actually achieved, can be lower or higher than the asking price.

used as helpful guidelines, BUT you shouldn't rely on them for an accurate estimate as the data could be several months old, so property prices could have moved up or down in that time. Use these estimates along with asking agents for recently sold comparables that haven't yet reached the 'sold' stage so you can secure the best research to help with your decision on what to offer or accept on your home.

Using property price surveys

One useful tool for assessing the overall upward or downward trend in property prices is the property price surveys, which are compiled by various companies. However, you must be careful not to use them as a guide to an 'average house price'. We often witness the media quoting property price surveys, which talk about an 'average house price'. You may think this refers to a three-bedroomed semi and

that the surveys compare the cost of this type of property across the country, but this is not the case. There is actually no such thing as an 'average' property when it comes to property price surveys.

What the property price surveys typically quote as an 'average property price' is a sum of all the properties they have in their database from which they obtain their 'average' price. However, some surveys include property that is sold for over £1 million while others don't. Some only cover mortgaged properties and omit those that might be sold and are owned outright, lowering the average property price that they quote versus other surveys.

They also vary so widely because they measure the market at different times of the property sale. For example, Rightmove measures the asking prices, whereas the Land Registry measures prices at the end of the transaction after any negotiations have taken place at survey or mortgage offer stage, which means they can be significantly lower. In addition, some surveys only cover England and Wales while others cover the whole of the UK, including Scotland and Northern Ireland.

The real value of property price surveys is to banks and other

Other sources for getting hold of local property market information are local newspapers, local estate agents and the internet. Each of these areas are explored on pages 84–6.

financial analysts who use them to assess consumer spending trends and the state of the economy. They also help the property services, such as estate agents and surveyors, to understand the impact on their business at a national level and to plan their staffing, sales and marketing initiatives.

To the general public, property price surveys can be helpful in providing information on how long it might take to buy or sell a property, whether the market is active and therefore you will have to make decisions more quickly, or if it is slow and you can therefore take your time. So effectively it gives a feel for how buyers are likely to react when you put your property up for sale. However, what surveys don't do is let you know what price you should market your property for, how much it has gone up (or down) in value since you last bought it, or how much you should offer. This depends on what is happening in the local market and the demand and supply for the property you are buying or selling. Property price survey information is available from the following companies.

Rightmove

This company has the widest range of all these surveys, collating information from more than 500,000 property sale details at any one time. The figures that they use only quote the 'asking price' or 'advertised price' for a property and so they can overestimate the real

prices achieved. For example, if a property is advertised at £300,000 but sells for £285,000, Rightmove will quote the higher figure. They release their data on a monthly basis and you can access the information at www.rightmove.co.uk.

Hometrack

Hometrack analyses data from over 3,000 estate agents in England and Wales. The company is widely regarded as the most useful survey because it compares asking prices with actual selling prices as well as assessing the demand and supply of properties in the area.

It also gives the average number of viewings for each sale and the average time a property is on the market. This helps you to

Self-fulfilling prophecies

Stories of housing market crashes are a favourite in parts of the media. However, despite the fact that they are often headline grabbing and the information then reported doesn't necessarily match the title, they can create the very effect they predict.

1 A paper runs a 'price crash' story, probably based on a selective interpretation of one survey.

2 Buyers read this and decide to wait for prices to fall so that they can get a better deal.

3 Visits and offers on properties drop, so the next month's figures show a less active market.

4 The surveys then record a slowdown of viewings and offers.

5 The media reports this 'slowdown' and says 'we told you so!'.

understand whether you are getting enough viewings to sell your home and whether you are behind your local market when it comes to selling. See www.hometrack.co.uk for regional statistics.

Halifax and Nationwide

Both of these companies take data from their mortgage lending businesses and so do not include the 25–30 per cent of property sales achieved without mortgages. Nevertheless, they are still valuable for showing national and regional price movements, and both allow you to put a price on your own property using their 'trend' data to estimate how much it is worth now versus when you bought it. However, it is only a guide, so don't rely on it.

Their information is released on a monthly basis for national information and a quarterly basis for regional information and can be accessed by visiting their websites: www.nationwide.co.uk/hpi and www.lloydsbankinggroup.com. On the Lloyds Banking Group website, click on the 'Media' tab, followed by the 'Economic Insight' tab and then open the pdf 'Halifax house price index' in the research list at the foot of the page.

RICS and the NAEA

The Royal Institution of Chartered Surveyors (RICS) measures data supplied by its 350+ surveyors and its prices take into account the condition of the property. The National Association of Estate Agents (NAEA) gives a good idea of the current supply and demand by showing how many properties agents have on their books. The higher this number, the harder properties will be to sell unless they really stand out.

Both organisations release information each month and you can access this by visiting their websites: www.naea.co.uk and www.rics.org.

The Land Registry

This survey covers actual transactions and the final price that someone pays for a property. This information is the most accurate of all the data and surveys, but the problem for buyers and sellers is that it is only released on a quarterly basis. So, as house prices can go up and down on a monthly basis, the Land Registry data is not especially helpful when you are buying and selling as it quickly becomes too historic and out of date.

Property price websites include: **www.communities.gov.uk**; **www.landreg.gov.uk**; **www.lloydsbankinggroup.com**; **www. naea.co.uk**; **www.nationwide.co.uk**; **www.propertycheck. co.uk**; **www.rics.org** and **www.rightmove.co.uk**.

Understanding your local property market

Understanding the local market for a property you want to buy or sell is far more important than any media reports on property price movements. There are many factors that can influence what is happening to property prices and how much you should offer or sell a property for.

> 'Understanding the local market for a property that you want to buy or sell is far more important than any media reports you might read on property price movements.'

Location

Local property markets are sub-divided into many sectors. For example, some streets are valued highly because they are adjacent to a park and so appeal to families with young children, or have plenty of parking, or are lined with beautiful trees. Others are worth less to some people because they have a pub that is notoriously noisy or the street is often strewn with litter from fast food outlets. As a result, it is important to understand the market and property type that you wish to buy or sell in your local area. For example, is there an over- or under-supply of old or new properties? What about easy access to shops? If there are only a few shops, then it is likely that properties within walking distance will be more expensive than those you have to drive from. Any properties on main or busy/noisy roads, for example, are likely to be cheaper than those set away from a road or in a quiet, idyllic location.

One of the biggest reasons for property price differences at a

Buying or selling?

Whether you are buying or selling or both, in the same or different areas, the advice on understanding the local market applies. As a seller, you need to make comparisons with properties similar to yours. As a buyer, you will want to study certain property types, and/or concentrate on your favoured locations.

Property market summary reports are available from **www. housepricecrash.co.uk** and **www.designsonproperty.co.uk**.

local level is the performance of schools. In some cases, property prices can be between 19 and 34 per cent higher than other areas due to a good school catchment area. However, be aware that not all local authorities and their schools have the same catchment area each year. Some vary the area according to local demand. The school may also be full and not accepting any new pupils, so if you are hoping to buy a property in a postcode to 'guarantee' a place for your children at a school, check with the school directly.

'One of the biggest reasons for property price differences at a local level is the performance of schools. In some cases, property prices can be between 19 and 34 per cent higher than other areas due to a good school catchment area.'

Economic

Is the area that you are buying or selling in expanding or contracting? For example, are companies moving into or out of the area? Are shops closing down due to lack of business or are they being turned into trendy outdoor cafés suggesting a new breed of professionals moving into the area?

Another good sign of economic development is if new properties are being built locally. Are the major house builders moving in? Are new estate agents opening up in the area? Perhaps there are run-down parts that are now being bought up and their buildings being turned into hotels, entertainment centres or executive flats.

These elements are not guaranteed to turn an area around or boost the property market in the long run, but they are definitely signs that things are on the up or down and therefore help you to understand whether prices are likely to rise or fall.

Transport links

Investment in local transport can impact dramatically on an area's fortune. For example, a new road or rail or tram link that means access to a major city or area of work may cut down travel from an hour to half an hour. Alternatively, lack of investment in transport and increased congestion can reduce prices as people try to move nearer to other modes of transport, or indeed decide to leave the area and live and work somewhere else.

Types of property and local demand

Each area will have new properties, flats, detached, semi-detached and terraced homes. Unfortunately, there is likely to be a glut of some properties and an under-supply of others. For example, in the lead up to the recession in 2007, developers built many flats and apartments for city centres. They were snapped up by some first-time or second-time buyers, but most by investors. Since the economic downturn investors' ability and willingness to purchase such properties has decreased and so the demand isn't as high as it was.

Character and old properties, particularly in idyllic country village locations that are still near to major towns or cities with good jobs, are always likely to be in short supply as many people want to live in them, but, unfortunately, supply cannot be increased. Hence some developers are trying to build properties with the 'character' of old ones, but the benefits of new builds.

Whenever you are looking to buy or sell a particular property in an area, make sure you talk to the local estate agents and surveyors and ask them what is the demand and supply for the type of property you are looking for or selling. In this way, you know that if demand is high, you will have to be prepared to offer more, or make a quick decision for a property you want to buy. Conversely, if demand is low and slow, you may have to take time and be patient in selling your home.

Local factors

There may be other factors locally that affect property prices, such as an area becoming well known for drug dealing, or indeed drug dealers being chased out of the area. We have already discussed the major impact that a good school can have on the price of property. However, it may be that a 'badly scored' school takes on a new head who over a few years turns the school around, which is likely to impact positively on the price of property in the area.

Some areas are well known, too, for problems with flooding, subsidence or radon. If you are not local, then always read the local newspapers as they will typically mention this over the time you are looking to purchase a property. If you are local, then you are likely to know which areas are affected and can make your own decision on

'Make sure you talk to local estate agents and surveyors and ask them what is the demand and supply for the type of property you are looking for or selling.'

For further information on facts that affect the local property market, see these websites: **www.environment-agency.gov. uk** (environmental); **www.homecheck.co.uk** and **http://maps. police.uk/** for crime in England and Wales.

how big an issue you feel it might be. Always check what effect this will have on your ability to get, or the cost of, insurance as an insurer won't always cover you (see pages 64–6).

Increasingly, crime has an impact on an area's price, but do check whether this is media hype or a real problem. One serious break-in, or worse, doesn't mean the whole place is awful to live in; it may have been a one-off occurrence. To get a sense of how much of an issue this is, check crime statistics or talk to the local police.

Insurance brokers are well worth talking to as well, as they will increase/decrease premiums according to the local crime rate. This can be particularly helpful if you are comparing two different properties in different postcode areas, as you may find the costs of insuring one property versus another are very different.

All of these factors will affect whether the price of property in a certain area is growing more or less than the average property prices quoted by the media. The better you understand these dynamics, the better you will be able to understand what might help you sell your home or if it is worth buying a property in an area.

'The better you understand the local area, the better you will be able to understand what might help you sell your home or if it is worth buying in that area.'

Comparing property prices

Local factors can affect property prices going up or down, but the demand and supply of individual properties can also cause the price of one property on one street to go up and the price of another around the corner to go down.

To explain how these prices can vary dramatically from one road to another, the table below shows how three different three-bedroomed semi-detached properties (new, Victorian and one built in the 1950s) will vary in price according to demand and supply and their appeal to people with contrasting requirements.

The new property could be worth around £180,000, the Victorian

property around £220,000 as it is a character property and in short supply, while the 1950s property might fetch around £160,000 as it's ex-local authority and some of the nearby properties are still social housing. All these properties could be within a few hundred metres of each other, yet the price difference for the same 'three-bedroomed property' could vary by over 35 per cent.

Comparison chart for different styles of property				
Properties with the same number of bedrooms (in this example, three), in the same area, can appeal to different markets, based on age and facilities.				
Age	**History/style**	**Location**	**Parking**	**Potential market**
New	Small terraced property	Suburban estate	Two spaces allocated	Working couple, both with company cars, eat out a lot and shop locally
Victorian	Semi-detached	Main road	None	Non-drivers, possibly a retired couple seeking easy access to public transport, doctors and hospitals
1950s	Ex-council	Cul-de-sac	Garage	Family with children, keen for them to be able to play safely nearby

In addition, if there are 20 people looking to buy a Victorian semi and there are only three on the market, the prices are likely to rise, while if a new release of 20 three-bed terraced properties are for sale and only five people are looking, the prices are likely to go down.

This example shows how important it is that you assess the property that you want to buy or sell in detail so that you understand why some 'similar' properties sell for more and others for less.

> 'Even in the age of the internet, it is worth keeping your eye on local newspapers to research the market.'

Sources for local property market information

To help you find out the demand and supply, and market conditions for a property you are buying or selling, there are many resources that you can now use.

Local newspapers

Even in the age of the internet, keep your eye on local newspapers to research the market. Some run a weekly report on trends in the area, but just by browsing through the advertisements, watching what sells and what doesn't, you will start to get an idea of what is available and the asking prices.

Look out for properties similar to yours. The asking prices will vary according to the location and condition of each property, but you may be able to make comparisons with your own. Make a note of the maximum and minimum prices properties are selling for and see if they change over a number of weeks (or ideally about three months). Try to work out why some are more expensive than others and how this impacts on the price of your own property. If you have time, have a look at them – you can tell a lot even from doing a

 Increasingly, local newspapers have websites so you can view local news and keep up to date with new properties coming on the market in the area. This is especially valuable if you are moving some distance.

'drive-by' of the property for sale. Factors affecting the price of individual properties include:

- Quiet location (or not)
- State of repair (paintwork on windows can be a good indicator – old and peeling exterior paintwork suggests lack of maintenance)
- Size of garden
- South-facing gardens are highly prized because they get more sun
- Conservatory
- Parking and/or garage
- What's next door.

Local estate agents

Local estate agents are another useful source of advice, particularly independent agents with a long history in the area. If you are selling, your dealings with them will help you in deciding how best to market your property and which agents offer the most professional service that is right for you (see pages 95–102). They should be able to tell you how long certain properties have been on the market, and how often certain types of property such as yours become available in the area.

If you are buying and show the estate agent that you are not a 'time-waster' (for example, by having a Mortgage Agreement in Principle ready, or if you are selling a property, already having it on the market), then they will often take time to talk to you about the market and explain the demand and supply for the particular property type that interests you. Try to see them on a day when they aren't too busy, as then they'll spend more time with you.

The internet

A major resource to research the value of your home – or how much to offer on the property you are looking to buy – is the websites that allow you to find the price that properties have actually sold for in the area you are selling or buying. You will obviously need to go online for this information. Some websites provide it for free, some require your email address and some charge for more comprehensive property price reports.

The advantage such websites have over newspapers is that they will search by postcode and often provide a map showing the location of the property. They also show the price that the property sold for – not what it was advertised at. This is particularly valuable if you have identified certain small areas,

The best websites to find figures for what properties have sold at are: **www.mouseprice.com** and **www.nethouseprices. com**. Some websites give access to information for free, others charge you per property.

even roads, where you would like to buy. It can, however, take up to three months for a particular property's details to appear, but you can look at property sold prices for an individual property up to six months ago to gain an idea of the true value of the type you are selling/looking for.

BE CAREFUL!

When there is a great deal of uncertainty over property prices, it is essential when pricing a property to only look at 'sold' property prices. In difficult conditions, properties that are overpriced will not get viewings, let alone an offer, so price realistically to ensure some viewings. When researching property prices online, always tick the box 'include sold properties' in the list of search requirements and find out how much these properties actually sold for.

'Websites will search by postcode – a big advantage over newspapers.'

Deciding what your home is worth

The table shown opposite combined with the research already outlined should help you to come up with a reasonable guide as to the value of a property you are going to buy or sell, unless it is a very unusual property with no local 'comparables'. In this case, you will need specialist advice from an estate agent or have to search the 'sold prices' information for a similar property that you know was sold in the last few years. Use the list to itemise the key points about the home you are looking to buy or sell and then compare them with those of similar properties.

Valuations by professionals

As soon as you have a good grasp of what is happening to property prices locally, you can turn to the professionals to help you value your home or sign up with the ones who are likely to sell the type of property you want. Whether or not you are going to use an estate agent (and most people do), it is worth asking them about the state of the market and how often the property you are selling or buying comes up for sale, and whether it will sell quickly.

Further specialist internet property sites are given on page 136. For more information on choosing a suitable agent and getting a valuation, see pages 95–9. These are both important decisions that can't be taken lightly and are the basis of a successful sale.

Property comparison information

Use this list to compare the details of the properties you are most interested in buying or, if you are selling, to make comparisons with your home.

Property price

Total square metres (this information is on the EPC report)

Property age

e.g. Brand new, post-war, pre-war, pre-1920

Type

e.g. Detached, semi, terraced, flat

Area

e.g. City centre, surburban, rural

Property specification

Number of bedrooms	Extension
Number of reception rooms	Loft conversion
Number of bathrooms	Double-glazing
Conservatory	Central heating

Condition

e.g. Well maintained, some minor work to do, major work required

Garden

e.g. Small, medium, large

Garage

e.g. Single, double, none

Price per square metre*

Useful analysis data

* Calculating the price per square metre (see box, overleaf) of a property is a useful analysis as sometimes a property can feel 'huge' versus another one with more, but smaller, rooms. It also helps to work out how much extra you pay for a better area, or having a garage and larger garden. Furthermore, it highlights how a potential buyer might assess your home versus others for sale in the area and, of course, you could use a similar table to compare the properties you are interested in buying.

Calculating the price per square metre

When you are making property comparisons (see page 87), use the property details or measure the rooms in your own home to calculate the price per square metre. Alternatively, check the property's Energy Performance Certificate (see pages 105–7) as this information is included in the top right-hand side of the report.

Dining room	3.6 x 3.6 metres = 12.96 square metres
Kitchen	3.6 x 2.4 metres = 8.64 square metres
Bedroom	3 x 2.4 metres = 7.2 square metres
Bathroom	1.8 x 1.2 metres = 2.16 square metres
Total square metres	30.96 square metres

Divide the value by the total square metres of the property's rooms. For example, if the property is worth £100,000, divide by 30.96 square metres, which equals £3,230 per square metre.

Over the course of buying or selling a property there are various prices that will be linked to your home. It is important not to get too 'attached' to one of them and refuse to negotiate: your home is ultimately only worth what someone else is willing to pay – and accept – for it.

So don't forget that even though you have accepted or had an offer accepted, the price of a property isn't necessarily guaranteed. The only time it is guaranteed is when contracts are exchanged as at that stage no more negotiation can take place without one party having to forfeit costs to the other.

Case study Richard

During the course of a house sale, its price can vary and this case outlines a not unusual chain of events.

Richard put his house on the market at £199,000 (price 1). A buyer duly offered £190,000 for it (price 2), but Richard had decided that he would only drop as far as £195,000 so negotiated the price up to that figure (price 3).

In came the surveyor, who found some damp, but as he felt the buyer was getting a good deal at £195,000 he still valued the property at that level. But the mortgage valuer found the same damp and recommended that it would cost £1,000 to put right, so she only valued the property at £194,000 (price 4).

Last, but not least, Richard and his buyer then had to negotiate a final price and they decided to 'split the difference' and so the selling price was agreed at £194,500 (price 5).

Selling your home

4

An important decision to make when selling your home is which (if any) estate agent to use: a choice that could have a major impact on how you sell your property. There is also guidance on good selling practice, and how to deal with any problems at this stage.

Getting yourself ready

If we sell our possessions, it's usually because we don't want or need them any more. If they have any emotional connotations, it is with the past.

Selling your home is different to selling possessions: it is part of your life, it is where you and your loved ones live, and (the point that can lead to major hold-ups later on) you probably bought it because you fell in love with it.

This emotional attachment to bricks and mortar is perfectly natural: the home shelters and protects us and is the setting for family life with all its ups and downs. At some level we can feel that by selling the home we are rejecting part of the family. This brings an emotional tinge to the selling process, which can be intensified by the reason for the sale. Separation, bereavement and retirement, for example, are major life events with related emotions yet are often the spur for a house sale, bringing a tangle of associations to a business transaction.

It is important that you recognise that you too are likely to have feelings about your property and that this can affect how you behave. Quite a lot of people take their property off the market at a late stage in proceedings because they suddenly realise they don't want to move after all. Someone who is harbouring such feelings is likely to be slow to deal with paperwork, unclear in their communication and generally hold things up in a subconscious bid to stop it happening at all.

> '**It is perfectly natural to have an attachment to bricks and mortar: our homes shelter and protect us and they are the setting for family life with all its ups and downs.**'

Chapter 2 (see pages 23-72) gives you advice on working out how much you can afford (a vital part of the process), and Chapter 3 (see pages 73-88) includes information on valuing a property.

But I love my home!

Once your home is on the market you will hear comments about it that you don't like. They might say that they dislike the décor, the way the rooms are laid out, the state of the garden or countless other things, which they'll forget in seconds and which could haunt you for years. Try to distance yourself from this and accept that the home you love could be someone else's nightmare.

Be clear about the money

Follow the information on how much you can afford in Chapter 2 (pages 23–72), and on property valuing in Chapter 3 (pages 73–88). This will help you set a maximum price that you would like to get for your house, and the minimum price that would still enable you to buy your next property. In the long journey ahead, keep both figures in mind, not just the maximum one: remember you are moving to live in a new home, not necessarily to make your fortune.

What will you sell?

Some fixtures and fittings are often included in the sale price. This includes curtains, carpets, door furniture and bathroom fittings, appliances, storage heaters and even sometimes the furniture itself. In every room, including the shed and the garage, decide on the following:

- What you are definitely taking with you.
- What you are prepared to negotiate over.
- What you definitely don't want. You will have to dispose of these items if your buyer does not want them either. It may be easiest to get rid of them now: less clutter means more space, and space sells property.

Think through whether you would want to sell anything that neither you nor your buyer wants. If you have bulky, unwanted items that you can't transport, your local council may be prepared to remove them for you for a small charge.

Write down the items, by room, for each category. Your estate agent and, later, your solicitor will need this information.

'Decide on a potential minimum selling price that would mean you could still afford to buy your next property.'

Jargon buster

Joint tenancy When two people own a property together and if one dies it automatically passes to the other, irrespective of the will.
GCH Abbreviation for gas central heating.

Get the paperwork ready

You will be asked to provide various items of paperwork at some stage. Get it all ready in advance and there won't be a big panic or delay when you have to find it. You will need:

- The buying information you were given when you purchased your house. Much of the information won't have changed (unless you have extended it or changed the layout, altering the room sizes).

- Any building regulations certificates for a new boiler, windows or planning permission information given if you have extended the property or it was extended before.

- Electrical certificates if you have had re-wiring done since January 2005.

- Any other documentation that you have from when you purchased your property.

- Current bills for Council Tax and supplies such as gas, electricity and water. This will allow you to demonstrate the running costs of the home.

- Buildings insurance, again for reference and because you will need to change this policy to your new property.

- Contents insurance, for the same reason.

- Mortgage roll or account number. You'll need this later, but some sales have been held up for weeks as the seller tries to track it down.

- Energy Performance Certificate. if you received one when you bought the property. For further information on EPCs, see pages 105–7.

Estate agents

Estate agents as a whole have had a poor reputation in the UK. This is now changing, especially as from 1 October 2008, all agents had to belong to an approved redress scheme.

Agents now have to abide by strict codes of conduct and, if they don't, you have an independent third party to address your complaints to for free.

If you sell your own house, you will save a substantial sum (the typical estate agent's fee is between 1.5 and 2 per cent, which pays £2,250–£3,000 on a £150,000 property). The drawback is the time and work that you will have to put in yourself. If you try but fail to sell your house, you won't save anything, but you still lose the time and the opportunity to move. For more information, see pages 103–4.

What does an estate agent do?

A good estate agent will visit your property and suggest three possible prices (see page 96, which includes other advice on what to ask them at this stage). Once you have chosen an agent and the price that you want to put it on the market for, the agent should:

- **Send you a contract** (see pages 100–3) setting out their terms and conditions. Read this before you sign.
- **Measure and photograph** the property to produce the sales particulars, checking them through with you.
- **Help you to secure an Energy Performance Certificate** (see pages 105–7 for further information). You don't have to use the agent to provide this service and they should charge around £50 for the certificate.
- **Put a 'For sale' board** outside your property (assuming you want one; your estate agent should give you the option).
- **Advertise your property** locally, on the internet and via newspapers. It's important to negotiate this as it doesn't always happen automatically.

→ The three suggested asking prices that an estate agent should give you are the asking price, a fair price and a lower price. For more information on this and how to make your decision for which price to go for, see pages 97-8.

- **Advertise it at their premises** and via their website as well as advertising directly to a list of potential buyers.
- **Arrange viewings** for legitimate buyers (and show people around your house if you aren't there).
- **Receive offers,** communicating them to you in writing and negotiating on your behalf.
- **Liaise** between your buyer, you and your solicitor.
- **Arrange** the handover of keys on completion day.

You could do most of this yourself. However, there are various benefits a good agent brings.

Experience

In any field, experience is something to be valued. Someone who has spent years helping people buy and sell property should be able to forestall problems, keep the process moving efficiently and effectively, and offer informed advice when decisions are required.

Property surveyors

Some estate agency practices are run by property surveyors and they tend to have a good feel of the overall market as they will be members of RICS and are likely to contribute to and receive their property price surveys (see pages 76–9). They also survey other properties locally, so tend to have a wider knowledge of individual local property prices.

Sales and marketing

Selling is a skill. No one is going to persuade an unwilling buyer to purchase your property, but a professional sales person will be able to communicate effectively, pointing out advantages and answering queries that might otherwise have put someone off. In addition, a good agent will have the resources to market your property nationally via their website.

Security

Inviting strangers into your home carries a risk. You don't know who they are and you can't vet them, but you could find yourself alone with them in your home. Sadly, these days this is not wise. An agent who accompanies viewers means that you won't be put in a vulnerable position.

Avoiding time-wasters

You can never be sure if a viewer is genuinely interested in your property, and some people make a hobby of looking around houses when they have no intention of buying. A good agent will check if the buyer is serious and ask if they have a Mortgage Agreement in Principle (see pages 40–1). If they haven't arranged a loan (which means there's no guarantee they can afford to buy), the agent can set this in motion.

Accessibility

Any decent agent will have someone available to talk to potential buyers. You might not be able to do this.

Get the best agent

When choosing an agent, read the advice on your local property market on pages 79–82 and only choose agents that you have checked are current members of one of two redress schemes. These are the Property Ombudsman and the Ombudsman Services: Property (see pages 97–100). This should give you an idea of which agents are not just marketing properties like yours, but selling them. In a high street with six agents, only two or three may be right for you, so always research by asking locals for recommendations. Also look at who is advertising properties like yours in the local paper and possibly on the internet. Estate agents tend to specialise. There is no point asbking one who usually sells large houses with land to market a small flat.

A common mistake when choosing an agent is the 'board count' method where potential sellers count how many boards (for sale and sold) and choose the agent with the most. However, there are some agents that offer high valuations to increase their market share, so they have the most boards. The only boards you should count should be the 'sold' boards as this gives a truer indication of success.

Choosing an estate agent in a difficult market

The last time property prices were stagnant, and even falling, was in the early 1990s. In a difficult market, it is essential to carry out thorough research to find the best agent. You need to find an agent who is very close to the local market and can pick up on any small movements – up or down. Ideally, choose an agent based on the number of similar properties to yours they have sold in the last year or two.

Jargon buster

Break clause When a sole agency can be terminated.

Mortgage Agreement in Principle An expression of a mortgage lender's willingness to enter into an agreement subject to other conditions being met. Also known as a MAP.

Property portal Website with properties from a variety of agents.

Property price surveys National surveys that study trends in the property market (see pages 75–9).

RICS Royal Institution of Chartered Surveyors.

Surveyor Qualified person who assesses the structural soundness of your home.

For further advice on finding an estate agent and what to do if your relationship with your estate agent breaks down, visit **www.which.co.uk/agentproblems**.

Location location

Just as the location of your house is important, so is the site of your estate agent. Your agent should be based in a town as near as possible to your property, and already be dealing in properties in your area. If your property is located between two towns, see which one has more agents who work in your area. If the split is equal, you may be better off using two agents (on a more expensive multiple agency deal – see page 100) because between them they will market your property more widely.

Check out where the agent's offices are. An upmarket location near a stylish clothes shop in the high street will attract different buyers to the one at the end of the street next to a scruffy pub or discount shop.

Get a valuation

Any decent estate agent will be willing to visit your house to make a free valuation. Invite three who have passed your initial checks described on page 95 to do this, asking them to bring details of any similar properties on the market or which they have sold in the last six months.

Walk around the property with the agent, inviting comments on any factors that will be attractive or not to potential buyers. This may help you see your property with fresh eyes, seeing the good points and spotting flaws, such as damaged doors, cracked plaster or peeling paper.

Who is your buyer?

What type of person is most likely to buy your property? An upmarket childless couple? A family with young children? An older person who wants to be near the shops? Now consider which agents appeal to that sector. Look at where they place advertisements and their style. Huge colour photographs of palatial residences won't attract someone looking for a bedsit: they're busy studying the page with small black-and-white pictures of flats.

Nothing structural

Agents are not surveyors and will not be looking for, or be trained to identify, any structural faults in the property. So discuss with the agent whether you should do either of the following.

- Have major repairs made before putting the house on the market.
- Get estimates in from builders so that you are equipped to negotiate from an informed standpoint.

A good estate agent will suggest that you consider the following three possible prices:

- **An asking price.**
- **A fair price** if you cannot achieve the asking price.
- **A lower price,** which is likely to help sell the property within two to six weeks.

Ask them their reasons for choosing each price. They may mention minor repairs like cracked window panes that you can easily fix and which have a big impact on the feel of a place. They will also know how many people are looking for properties of this type, and that will certainly affect the asking price. Ask them how many properties they have had on the market in the last 12 weeks and how many of those have actually sold.

Going through this process with three agents will give you a good idea of the likely asking and final selling price. If the price range differs by more than 5 per cent, talk to a couple more agents.

Making your decision

Overleaf there are a suggested list of questions to ask your potential agents, which will help you narrow down your choice of which agent to go with.

Ombudsman schemes

Since October 2008, two redress schemes have been formed and estate agents must belong to one of these schemes. The two schemes are the Property Ombudsman (www.tpos.co.uk) and the Ombudsman Services: Property (www.ombudsman-services.org). Members of these schemes must keep an accurate written record of their client interaction for six years. If you have a complaint to make, this makes it easier for you to resolve as there is an independent third party that will handle your complaint – for free!

Both schemes require agents to follow a code of conduct.

BE CAREFUL!
When choosing your asking price, remember that just as £4.99 is a more attractive price than £5.00, so £149,950 seems a far more attractive price than £150,000.

If an agent fails to do this and subsequently doesn't handle your complaint to your satisfaction, you can refer them to one of the ombudsman schemes.

The code of conduct covers areas that can cause problems between agents, buyers and sellers. These include the need to fairly represent the value of your property, to provide clear contracts and to give a full explanation of agent fees prior to you instructing an agent to act on your behalf. For example, agents should make it clear to you that if you dis-instruct them and then go on to sell to a buyer they introduced within six months, you may nevertheless be liable for their fee.

According to the Property Ombudsman, most of the issues that now arise between agents and buyers or sellers are communication problems, so it is essential to ensure that you take time to read an agent's terms and conditions before you sign and ask for key costs in writing. If you are not happy with anything during your sale or purchase, put your complaint or query in writing so there is a record that can be forwarded to one of the ombudsman schemes should you need to involve a third party.

Key questions to ask an estate agent

- How many similar properties have you sold?

- What prices did they achieve?

- How long did they take to sell?

- How many viewings did it take to gain a sale?

- How many buyers have you got looking in my price range?

- When you mail out my details, how many will you mail out to?

- Are any of your buyers in a cash or sold position?

- Will you advertise my property all the time in your window?

- Will you advertise my property in the local property newspaper every week?

- Which property portals do you advertise on? (For example, do you use Rightmove?)

- Who will deal with my property? (If possible, have a chat with that person.)

- Will you only send viewers who already have their loan finance sorted out?

- How might you deal with any problems (for examples, see pages 120–2)? (A good agent can help to keep the process moving smoothly.)

- Which redress scheme do you belong to?

- Are you a member of any other associations?

- What estate agency qualifications have you/your staff got?

- Can I see a copy of your terms and conditions?

- What if I want to market my property privately too? (You need a 'sole agency' agreement; see page 100.)

- What charges do you make apart from your agency fees?

- If I give you sole agency, how long will I be locked into a contract? (It is best to have a break clause after six or eight weeks, when you can go to another agent if you wish.)

- If you are not introducing buyers or getting offers, can I break the contract?

- If I have a complaint, how is it handled? Are you a member of the Property Ombudsman (see box, below)?

- How many different members of staff will help buyers view the property?

- Will you accompany buyers on all the viewings?

- Do you do weekend and evening viewings?

- What procedures do you have to follow up after a viewing?

- How do you check that buyers can afford my property?

- Are floor plans and pictures included in the property details?

- Have you got a sales progression department that will chase the chain?

Codes of practice

From 1 October 2008 all estate agents have had to belong to an approved redress scheme, so there will always be a third party that will independently handle your complaint. The Property Ombudsman (www.tpos.co.uk) and the Ombudsman Services: Property (www.ombudsman-services.org) are approved for the redress scheme. Estate agents may also belong to other trade organisations with their own codes of practice, such as the Royal Institute of Chartered Surveyors (www.rics.org) and the National Association of Estate Agents (www.naea.co.uk).

The contract

You can avoid many potential problems by reading the estate agent's contract, making sure you understand it and re-negotiating anything you don't like before you sign it.

Many disputes between sellers and agents stem from misunderstanding the contract. If you don't understand the contract, don't sign it: you may be better off with a different agent. Always read the contract carefully and look for the following terms.

Sole, joint or multiple agency

■ A 'sole selling agent' will have the exclusive right to sell your property and will be paid, even if you find a buyer yourself. However, it is important to negotiate this beforehand in writing and check the terms as not every agent will do this.

■ A 'sole agency' is still the only agent, but they don't get paid if you find a buyer.

■ Both of these will cost less than joint (two) or multiple agents, who will charge a higher commission rate to compensate for the fact that only one of them will get paid. See page 96 for advice on when it can be worth having more than one agent.

Make sure the contract clearly states that you won't be charged commission if the sole agency contract has ended.

The fee

Estate agents charge a percentage, plus VAT, of the final selling price. Rates vary, but they are typically 1.75 per cent for sole agency, and 2–3.5 per cent for multiple or joint arrangements.

These rates are negotiable, but remember the agent has been through this process more times than you have. It is worth asking the estate agent how much in real terms the fee could be, this will help you to draw up a budget.

 See the information on property price surveys in Chapter 3 (pages 73–88) to gain more of an idea of the potential value of your property. This will help you when choosing which estate agent you will go with.

Ready, willing and able purchaser

If the contract contains a term stating 'ready, willing and able purchaser', walk away – don't sign any contract with it. It will mean that you'll still have to pay the estate agent for finding you a buyer even if your situation changes and you have to withdraw from the sale.

Payment

Choose an agent that gives you a few days for the money to transfer before charging interest. And make sure it requires payment when the sale is completed rather than when contracts are exchanged. Do not hand over the authority to pay the estate agent to anyone else (known as irrevocable authority

BE CAREFUL!

If you know of someone that might be interested in your property, but still want to put it on the market with an agency, tell the agent (in writing) that you may have a private buyer before you sign the contract. If the private buyer, dealing direct with you, subsequently purchases your property, you will not be liable to pay the estate agent a fee.

– you should avoid this). If you have a complaint about the service provided, you won't have the power to withhold payment.

Tie-in periods

Avoid lengthy tie-in periods of anything over eight to twelve weeks. You should also remember to factor in the notice period, which is often two weeks – you can't usually give notice until the minimum contract period is over.

Open-ended agreements

Check what happens when the contract ends. Some agents operate a 'six-month rule' whereby you have to pay them if a buyer they introduced buys your home within six months of a contract ending. But some agents go further and state that you have to pay this, no matter how long it is after the termination of a contract.

BE CAREFUL!

If the agent tries to charge a 'fixed fee', even if it is expressed as a percentage of the asking price (not the selling price): it means they'll bill you for that fee no matter what the property actually sells for. This is bad value if your price drops, but can be a good deal if the fee is set at a lower percentage of a highly priced property.

Websites for relevant trade associations are: **www.naea.co.uk** (National Association of Estate Agents), **www.tpos.co.uk** (The Property Ombudsman) and **www.rics.org** (Royal Institution of Chartered Surveyors).

Your rights when dealing with an agent

It's your legal right that estate agents must do the following:

■ **Pass on all offers on a property.** There have been cases where offers have not been passed on to the vendor simply because a person making a lower offer hasn't agreed to use the estate agent's mortgage services.

■ **Pass on offers promptly** in writing. They shouldn't just telephone you to inform you of an offer.

■ **Use clear contract terms.**

■ **Reveal to you** any financial interest that they have in offers made on your property. For example, they are not allowed to collude with property developers so that the only offers they pass on to you are those that suit their interests.

If you suspect that an agent has acted in breach of these regulations, you should contact the local authority trading standards department together with the redress scheme they are a member of and professional association, if they are a member.

'Some agents will charge a fee if a buyer they found buys your home within six months of a contract ending.'

Selling your property yourself

If your research into the local market reveals that demand for property of your type is high, and houses seem to be selling quickly, suggesting a buoyant market, why not try to sell your property yourself?

This is a particularly good idea if you already know someone who wants to buy it – a friend or contact, or perhaps someone who put a note through the letterbox asking if you were interested in selling.

If you sell your property yourself, you will certainly save a big chunk of money – but buyers will be aware of this and consequently may try to negotiate a lower price to share in the saving. If your property has a complicated leasehold situation or if ownership is disputed, don't try selling it yourself.

How can you sell your own property?

About eight out of every ten property buyers are already local (within five miles), so you need to spread the word in your area. Tell your friends and contacts and put up a 'For sale' board (see box, right).

You'll need to prepare sales particulars for potential buyers and to remind viewers of what your property was like. Although this information is not subject to the Property Misdescriptions Act (which applies to particulars prepared by estate agents), it must be accurate.

The information you should include is:
- **Interior and exterior** photographs.
- **A floor plan** if possible (often a major selling tool).
- **A general description** followed by room-by-room details (see box on page 104).
- **Details of what is included** in the sale (such as curtains and any appliances), the Council Tax band and cost, and the asking price and your contact details.

BE CAREFUL!

There are legal requirements about 'For sale' boards. You can only use one up to 0.5 square metres, or two joined together to a maximum of 0.6 square metres. They must have a different advertisement on each side. Remember also that they need to be securely positioned – you don't want them clobbering a potential buyer (or anyone else!).

Room by room

The description should include a concise room-by-room guide to the house, text for each room stating its size (in metres), the number of windows, telephone, radiators, electric and TV cable points and other points of interest, such as open fireplaces or fitted wardrobes. Imagine the route you will take to show buyers, and follow this room order in the particulars.

Look at the particulars on other properties from a range of estate agents to help you with the style and content of your own particulars.

You could place advertisements in the local press, but they are unlikely to attract the attention achieved by the large colour spreads of the agents. You can get a reasonable-sized advert for £150 or more. However, smaller local publications, such as parish newsletters, are a cost-effective possibility, as are advertising-only papers, such as Loot and Dalton's Weekly. Another route is private property sale websites, such as www.propertybroker.co.uk and www.propertyweb.co.uk. You could also create your own advertisement to place in newsagents and other local shops, companies and offices, and sports and social clubs – anywhere with a noticeboard where you're allowed to put up an advert.

New internet initiatives

One of the problems to date with selling a property yourself is that many buyers search for property online first. The successful property portals so far are typically supportive of agents, so it has been difficult to gain the same level of exposure. This is partly why only a few private sale websites have been very successful.

What if you don't sell?

If you don't sell your property or gain any interest within 8-12 weeks, you may need to swallow your pride and use an estate agent. It may be worth considering taking it off the market for a while first, before putting it back on sale through an agent.

Energy Performance Certificates

In May 2010 Home Information Packs (HIPs), which had been required in England and Wales, were suspended by the coalition government. Energy Performance Certificates (EPCs), which were previously part of HIPs, are still required.

When you put up your property for sale, although you will no longer need to pay up to £350 for a HIP in England and Wales, you will still need to have an EPC to market your home for sale. Rules are different in Scotland, so if this is relevant to you, see pages 186–8.

This certificate is a physical inspection of your property and shows how energy efficient your home is. In a new home, this is likely to be good as most developers use the latest methods. If you have an older home with no insulation or double glazing, the performance rating is likely to be low.

The EPC shows your property's efficiency in a similar way to a fridge – your property is scored on a scale of A to G, with A being the best performance. The certificate gives an estimate of the costs for gas and electricity and includes recommendations to make your new home more efficient.

If the home is new, and you are buying off plan (so it's not yet built), then you will be provided with a 'predicted' assessment and a final certificate will be given when the property is complete. When buying, EPCs are very useful as they highlight the property's size in square metres as well as indicating how much it costs to heat the property and what action you can take to reduce utility bills.

If the property has been let since 1 October 2008 in England and Wales, 31 December 2008 in Northern Ireland and 1 January 2009 in Scotland and Ireland, it may already have an EPC. Check with a local estate agent, but you should be able to use this for the sale as they are valid for ten years.

Are you up for a Green Deal?

The Green Deal is a new initiative that the Government is enabling to

To find out more about an EPC go to to the Directgov website at **http://epc.direct.gov.uk**.

encourage you to make your home energy efficient.

The main feature of the Green Deal is the creation of a new financial product. This allows you to take out a new type of loan via your property's energy meter, to implement changes such as solid wall insulation or installing a new boiler.

To take up the Green Deal, you will need to seek impartial advice from a qualified energy assessor who will make recommendations via a Green Deal Plan based on average savings your property type could make. Once implemented, the cost of the energy saving measures will be paid for via your electricity bill, based on these average savings.

You will need to ensure the Green Deal Plan is given by a registered company. Any problems following the implementation of the deal will be dealt with by the company used, or, if needed, the Energy Ombudsman Service.

Ordering an EPC

EPCs have to have been ordered by the date that your property is marketed. There are several ways of doing this, either buying direct from a domestic energy assessor, by going online or buying one via your estate agent or letting agent.

Prices can vary dramatically, so it's worth shopping around as some companies will charge as little as £45 while others will charge as much as £100.

Domestic energy assessors (DEAs)

The person that issues an EPC is called a domestic energy assessor (DEA) and it is important to ensure that he or she is:

- **Qualified** with an ABBE Level 3 Diploma in Domestic Energy Assessment, granted by the Awarding Body for the Built Environment.
- **Accepted** as a member of a government-approved accreditation scheme, like the NHER accreditation scheme.
- **Accredited** via the Domestic Energy Accreditation Scheme (www.nesltd.co.uk/content/dea-accreditation)

An EPC and sellers

At the moment, while utility prices are not high enough to be a factor for most people when buying a home, many people just have the EPC done and don't even concern themselves with reading it. However, this may change in the future as energy prices rise over time.

As a result, there is nothing

The Energy Accreditation Scheme website is **www.nesltd.co.uk/content/ dea-accreditation** where the is also more information about the NHER accredication scheme. Green deal companies will be accredited by Gemserve and the Energy Ombudsman Service.

in particular you need to do as a result of having an EPC carried out. However, it is worth noting that if your property is given a rating of 'C' or above, that it is more energy efficient than most other properties for sale, so it can be used as a selling point as the utility bills a buyer will have to pay will be less.

If you have done work on the property to achieve this rating (by design or accident!), it is worth ensuring that this is pointed out to buyers in the property marketing details and when they visit. For example, if you have recently had your loft insulated to current standards (see the Energy Saving Trust, below, for more information), you may be passing on savings to the new home owners of up to £150 per year in heating bills. New installations of double glazed windows and also fitting energy-saving light bulbs can help to promote your home as a 'green home' to buyers, which is something they may not previously have considered.

An EPC and buyers

Currently, EPCs are not really taken that seriously by most buyers, which can be shortsighted as with heating bills likely to rise, the more energy efficient a home is, the lower

'**Currently, EPCs are not taken that seriously by most buyers, which can be shortsighted as with heating bills likely to rise, the more energy efficient a home is, the lower your utility bills will be.**'

your utility bills will be. The EPC assessment and ratings will give you an idea and estimate of how much it will cost to run a home.

If you do take time to read the EPC and want to keep your heating bills as low as possible, it is worth noting down what you would need to do to the property to make it more energy efficient and check with the Government's Energy Saving Trust what it will cost and what savings you could make over time. For example, it might, with a government grant, only cost £100 to have the loft insulated, but if this saves you £50 (or more) a year on your heating bills and you stay in the home for the average seven years, that's £100 expense in return for 7 x £50 = £350 savings. Better still, it could be an opportunity to negotiate money off the price of the property, so you don't even need to spend the initial £100.

The Energy Saving Trust is a government organisation that provides free and impartial advice on how to stop wasting energy - go to **www.energysavingtrust.org.uk** for more information.

The legal process

The legal aspect of your house sale must be carried out to the letter, or the whole process could fall through. Don't leave finding a conveyancer until you have a buyer: sort it out in advance, thereby saving time and hassle.

Conveyancing usually takes from six to twelve weeks, but paperwork delays can significantly hold up the selling process. Make sure that you read everything you are sent, and deal with it as quickly as possible, returning it by hand or registered post. If there's anything you don't understand, pick up the phone or email your legal company.

'To help keep your conveyancing time as short as possible, deal with all the paperwork as promptly as you can.'

Choose a legal firm

You need to use either a solicitor or a licensed conveyancer. All solicitors are qualified to do this work, but it is a specialist job so make sure whoever you go to is experienced in this field. Costs vary widely, and there are some very good internet-based providers or use online calculators (see box, below). Internet providers will mainly have a solicitor panel they will give your work to. They will give you access to your case over the internet and text you updates and you can deal with the solicitor allocated in whatever way you wish, many of which operate on fixed fees. A no completion, no fee service is also offered. Most of the information comes via email, so your conveyancer doesn't have to be local (although it might save time on occasion, and you might

 Internet-based providers to consider using include **www.1stpropertylawyers. co.uk** or use online calculators such as **www.homemoverquote.com**.

feel more confident that you can keep things moving if they are on your doorstep). Check out the following points:

- **The firm or department** specialises in conveyancing.
- **The person handling your work** isn't due to go on holiday or, if they are, who will cover for them.
- **They know your preferred exchange and completion date** and can work to it. Some conveyancers handle hundreds of cases at a time so make sure they have a limit to the number they choose – it should be no more than 100 and you want to be on the top of their pile.
- **Ask about charges.** These vary a lot. The cheapest may not be the best.

See also the 'seven questions' initiative, which offers advice on choosing a legal firm: www.adviceguide.org.uk.

Instruct your legal firm

You will need to 'instruct' a legal company to carry out your conveyancing as soon as you have agreed an offer on your home – so it makes sense to find one that you are happy with ahead of this. As long as you are sure you are going to sell your home, choose your conveyancer as soon as you put your house on the market. In this way you can give your solicitor time to prepare contracts and get the necessary details from

---

Jargon buster

Conditions of sale Part of the contract of sale (see page 111).

Conveyancing The legal and administrative process involved in transferring the ownership of a loan on any building from one owner to another.

Deeds Documents conferring and evidencing ownership of land.

Fixed fee You only pay the conveyancer's fee that is agreed at the outset.

Fixtures and fittings form A form sent to you by your conveyancer requesting information relating to fixtures and fittings (see page 111).

No sale, no fee An agreement with your conveyancer that does just that – if there's no sale, they won't charge you a fee (see page 22 for exceptions).

Particulars of sale Part of the contract of sale (see page 111).

Property information form A form sent to you by your conveyancer requesting specific information relating to your property (see page 111).

'Choose your conveyancer once you have put your property on the market so that you are prepared for prompt action once you have agreed a sale.'

Do it yourself?

You can do your own conveyancing but there's less incentive these days as the introduction of specialist firms has cut fees. You can buy the documents from a legal stationer and fill them in yourself, then apply to the Land Registry for the other documentation needed. It's time-consuming, calls for a good eye for detail and mistakes could land you in court.

On the other hand, you'll know everything that's going on and the reason for any delays and you'll save on fees and mark-ups on costs. Conveyancing for new houses or flats is more complicated than for other property types. You can pay a solicitor to check your paperwork once you have done it – they'll charge around £100 for this. Some mortgage lenders will not accept you purchasing a property (with their money!) without a legal representative.

roll/account number. They can ask for the deeds from the lender (unless you already have them) and draw up a draft contract. Getting this organised ahead of a sale can save around six weeks delay further down the line.

Bear in mind that getting together legal paperwork and then wading through it can take days of your time. Save time when buying and selling by drawing up a draft contract of sale as soon as you put your property on the market'.

Go for no sale, no fee and fixed fee

Busy conveyancers with too many cases on their desk are forced into a 'fire fighting' approach: they pick up a file that's due to exchange, realise something is missing, request it, and won't chase it for a week. Delays can lead to failed contracts. 'No sale, no fee' deals give them an incentive to get the job done quickly because it reduces the chances of hold-ups and they are more likely to get paid for finishing the job. Most 'no sale, no fee' firms also offer 'fixed-fee' conveyancing, which means you only pay the price you sign up to, so the more efficient they are, the more likely they are to make a profit. This is potentially the opposite for those that charge by the hour!

you. When a buyer is found, all contract documentation can be sent immediately.

They will require proof of identity, such as a passport or birth certificate, a marriage certificate if the property is jointly owned, plus proof of your address, such as a recent utility bill. Once they have this, they will also need your estate agent's details and your mortgage

Fill in the property information and fixtures and fittings forms

You will be sent a questionnaire by your conveyancer requiring information on:

■ Your mortgage
■ Who owns the various boundaries of the property
■ Any disputes with neighbours
■ The mains services available
■ Copies of any guarantees (such as for damp courses, wiring, plumbing or timber treatment) or planning permission, building regulation certificate or Part P certificate for electrical changes and a Gas Safety certificate for changes to any gas, including a new boiler.

There will also be a form setting out the fixtures and fittings that are included in the sale. You may not yet know which of these are included, so confirm what you can and mark the rest 'TBC' for 'to be confirmed'.

After an offer is agreed

Once you have accepted an offer, your representative will contact your buyer's solicitor to check on what stage they are at with their house sale and obtaining a mortgage. Tell your solicitor of any conditions of the sale, such as an agreed time to complete, and supply dates for when you want to exchange and complete.

Read and sign the contracts

Your legal company should draw up your contract of sale within a matter of weeks of you instructing them. Ask for the contract and read it carefully before signing. It will be in two parts:

■ **The particulars of sale,** which describe the property and give the terms of the lease or freehold.
■ **The conditions of sale,** which include the proposed completion date and what deposit is required on exchange of contracts.

Your legal firm will send an identical contract to the buyer's solicitor at the same time together with copies of the title deeds.

Answer your buyer's questions

Often at this stage the buyer's representative will have questions about your property. Answer these as quickly as you can. This is frequently the biggest cause of

'Put in writing any questions you need answered about the property. Ensure your legal representative then deals with them well in advance of exchange.'

delay for exchange. It is what the conveyancer forgets to 'ask for' in advance, or what the buyer's legal company forgets to answer. Some companies have standard questions they send out, which can be done automatically. You should ensure that you put in writing any questions you need answered about the property and ensure your legal representative asks them well in advance of exchange.

Agree the deposit

Deposits from the buyer used to be straightforward. If you bought a property for less than £100,000, then you would pay 5 per cent at the time of exchange and for £100,000+ a 10 per cent deposit. However, with the recent history of property price rises from early 2000, many purchasers just don't have the cash

> '**Completion dates are typically set within two weeks of exchange, but you can ask for more time if needed.**'

to pay the 10 per cent, so some legal companies are accepting a 5 per cent cash deposit at time of exchange.

Exchange contracts

Once the contracts are signed and the deposit has been paid, the legal companies phone all interested parties to confirm. Both parties are now legally committed to the purchase.

Completion dates are typically set two weeks after exchange, but they don't need to be. If no one in the chain is in a hurry to move, you can ask for more time. Four weeks or more means you have greater time to organise removals, ditch what you don't need to take with you, pack what you want to yourself, organise new works for your home and change of address information. A longer exchange to completion date can remove a lot of the stresses of buying and selling a home. This is particularly helpful

BE CAREFUL!

As soon as (and never before) you hear that the money has been paid in, you can hand over the keys. To avoid a potentially embarrassing conversation on your doorstep where you (rightly) refuse to hand over the keys to the buyer, leave them with the estate agent, who will then not release them without your or the legal company's say-so.

Stamp Duty Land Tax (SDLT) is now paid on properties sold for more than £125,000. See page 22 for the rising scale of SDLT.

if you haven't moved for ten or more years.

This is also a good time to check that you don't owe any money to the mortgage lender or the loan company who lent you money based on your property, if you are selling for less than the money you owe.

BE CAREFUL!

If you are only paying a 5 per cent deposit on a £100,000+ property and the sale falls through after exchange and so doesn't complete, you are still likely to have to pay the full 10 per cent deposit.

Reach completion

The final balance to make the purchase is paid to your solicitor on completion day. If you are part of a chain, all these payments will be made one after the other.

Re-register title deeds

Your legal company can help you register the change of ownership within five weeks of completion at which point you are liable to pay the stamp duty.

Case study Mr and Mrs Cooper

Always ask for proof at the outset that someone can afford to purchase your property. Mr and Mrs Cooper put their home up for sale in a small town by the sea. They were looking to move to a larger property so their children could have more room, and they both needed office space.

They put their home up for sale in February and gained an offer within the first two weeks, having sensibly priced the property and placed it with a well-known local agent. Sadly, the sale didn't proceed far after offers were confirmed and, after some more weeks, the buyers pulled out – without giving any reason.

Sensibly, they had kept the property on the market and soon another buyer was found, this time a cash buyer, or so they said! Only a few weeks later, it turned out they couldn't raise the funds for the property. A few months later a third 'cash' buyer turned up but, again, the vendors were out of luck. It turned out that the latest buyers couldn't sell their holiday let.

At this stage, Mr and Mrs Cooper nearly gave up, but had found a property to buy with a very understanding couple. So Mr and Mrs Cooper accepted this third 'cash' buyer but kept their house on the market just in case they could find yet another buyer. Surely not? But yes, another offer came through and this couple wanted to move fast, within a few weeks!

This time the vendors asked for a Mortgage Agreement in Principle and the purchasers had their solicitors already lined up. Exchange was eventually reached. So, don't forget – get that proof; lack of funding is the biggest reason for sales falling through after offers are made.

Selling your home

Most people selling and buying at the same time tend to concentrate on buying, but you should be looking at your home as if you were a potential buyer. For example, start with looking at it from the outside – how does it look?

Increasingly, potential buyers drive around an area and check out properties that are on the market before they make an appointment to view. So, look at your home with a view to:

- **Is it tidy?**
- **Does anything need repairing** that makes the property look uncared for? What about those little jobs like fixing an outside dripping tap or painting the windows?
- **Are the windows clean?**
- **Does the front door** look smart? (First impressions are crucial.)
- **Does the front garden** look cared for? Does the grass need a cut?

> **'Look at your home as if you were a potential buyer.'**

Preparing your home

Take a tour your home, walking through all the rooms and looking at them with fresh eyes. Doing this with an estate agent when they are valuing can help here. Ask them if there is anything you need to improve or change.

Know your buyer

If your property is likely to appeal to a first-time buyer, you could include appliances, curtains and carpets in the asking price as this will make it more attractive. If your target buyer is a family with young children, make it clear where pushchairs can be stored, and if you haven't got play equipment in the garden, put some in so it looks like a friendly space. If yours is a two-bedroom house with a box room suitable as a nursery, put a cot or small bed in it to show it fits.

In addition to the other checks for estate agents (see pages 98–9), ensure the particulars about your property are accurate. Sometimes confusion has arisen because the property may need re-decorating but be presented on the particulars as requiring modernising, implying more work is required than is the case.

Be accurate!

Make sure your EPC is accurate by taking time to prepare for the visit from the energy assessor. For example, know the thickness of your loft insulation and have ready receipts of work you have done to reduce the property's CO_2 emissions. Always ask the energy assessor if there are any improvements you can make prior to sale to help you reduce the cost of heating bills. Good preparation could lead to a better rating.

Tone it down

Buyers need to be able to picture themselves living in your home. This is much easier to do when the setting is neutral and uncluttered. If your walls are a bright pink, paint them a softer colour. Strong colours put buyers off. Also get rid of any mould, grease, grime or limescale in bathrooms and kitchens.

Make a feature

Every room can benefit from having a memorable feature that makes it seem different to the rest. This could be a stained glass window or a lovely fireplace. If there isn't one, add a vase of flowers or a similarly striking accessory.

Create space

Buyers like to see large, airy, spaces: it's easier for them to imagine where their furniture will go. So clear out furniture or fittings that you no longer need. It will also save you money when you are booking or organising your removals.

Keep it tidy

Clutter puts buyers off. So get as many of your possessions as possible out of the way, into storage, the roof space or cupboards. Keep on top of the washing-up, too, so that a buyer isn't faced with a pile of dirty pans in the sink.

Be positive

However desperate you are to sell, and whatever reservations you may have about your property, smile and find positive things to say about it: the atmosphere you create will influence how people feel about your home.

Take precautions

Don't show the property to viewers on your own unless you have some kind of proof of their identity, such as a landline number or address. In fact, if there is no agent present when showing a viewer around, ask a friend or relative to be present. Make sure someone else knows you have an appointment and who it is with. Keep valuables out of sight.

If you are arranging viewings yourself, get a landline phone number and ring them back to make the appointment (you can say you need to check timings with your partner).

Arranging viewings

Your agent will arrange viewings. You will usually have at least a few hours', and possibly days', notice, but sometimes you'll get a phone call asking if they can pop around in a few minutes because it suits the buyer's schedule. Try to be gracious about this because you don't know which viewing is going to lead to a sale.

Some people prefer to let the agent show buyers round. Others feel they will do a better job of pointing out the good features of their own home themselves. You might end up showing people around at weekends, but leaving weekday appointments while you are at work to the agent.

Most properties look their best in daylight. Avoid mealtimes as buyers will feel uncomfortable watching the rest of your family eat, and will shorten their visit. Also, cooking smells can put people off.

If you do find it difficult to keep everything clean and tidy, then ask your estate agent about an 'open day'. It's something that is done often in Australia and can be quite effective. Basically the 'open day' is advertised and times given, then a series of bookings are made by the agent at, say, half-hourly intervals. The upside is that an open day makes it much easier for you, the slight downside is that it restricts when buyers can come. However, having an open day does give a key 'date' for people to view your property and may help gain a sale, or even competitive bids.

What to say and do

Before showing anyone around, think of things you like about each part of your home. Some ideas are:

- **Exterior:** Convenient parking, helpful neighbours, a well-planted garden.
- **Kitchen/utility:** The lovely view from the kitchen window where you can watch the children playing in the garden, a good spot to leave dirty boots.
- **Living room:** The way you can dim the lights to change the mood, the high ceiling that gives a sense of space, or the low beams that add character and cosiness, the view it offers of the sunset.
- **Bedrooms:** The fact that they can take a double bed, the fitted wardrobes, the morning sunlight, the convenient en suite.
- **Bathrooms:** The elegant taps, the generously sized mirror, the sense of space.

BE CAREFUL!

Agents usually ask for a set of keys so they can carry out viewings when you are out. You may also need to tell them how any alarm system works. If this is the case and you can't be in for viewings, ask for a copy of their key-handling policy. Some agents do not have a good security system for keys, and there have been cases of burglaries where keys left with estate agents have been used to enter properties and steal from them.

These show your home's advantages over similar properties. It is worth trying to work them into the conversation (not reciting them from a clipboard) and it gives you something to say other than, 'This is the lounge.' Type or write out the top ten points and give them to your agent so they can refer to them when they are conducting viewings.

People expect to come in through the main entrance, so even if you usually come in through the back door, welcome them at the front. If they have not got a set of sale particulars, offer them one, with a pen to make notes. It is usually best to start the tour in the living room. Complete the rest of the downstairs area before moving upstairs. Then go out into the garden (have a couple of umbrellas handy in case of rain). At the end of the tour, ask if they felt what they have seen matched the particulars, and how they have found dealing with the agent. This allows them to give you information, which may help you market your property better, and you'll probably get an impression of how they feel about your home, too.

Information to keep and give out

This is something many sellers don't do, but it all helps.

- **Have copies** of the particulars of sale for reference.
- **Have a copy** of the EPC (see pages 105–7).
- **Keep examples of recent bills** (cross out confidential details such as account numbers) so that you can show running costs.
- **Have a copy of the local paper** as it helps give an impression of the area to outsiders.
- **Create a list of local** doctors, dentists, parks, playgroups, primary and secondary schools, libraries and anything else you think is useful (gear it to your potential buyer).
- **The nearest** leisure and shopping centres.

First impressions

First impressions count. Buyers make decisions about whether they are interested in a property within seconds of their arrival. Making them feel comfortable makes it more likely they will view it in a positive frame of mind. Be polite, even if this is a surprise viewing that is delaying your shopping trip. Try not to appear over desperate to sell: it suggests either a problem, or an opportunity to negotiate the price down.

A part of your agent's job is to telephone buyers a few days after the viewing to ask what they thought of it and if they have any questions or would like to view again (see page 99). Feedback is useful as it will help you achieve a sale by changing things that put buyers off.

- **Menus of local restaurants** and takeaways give a feel for the locality and highlight convenience or exclusivity.
- **Local bus and train timetables** will be valuable to commuters or those who don't drive.

Vetting a buyer and their offer

If someone makes an offer, there are a number of things to consider apart from the money.

- **Are they a first-time buyer?** If so, your chain might be quite short (depending on who you are buying from), which is a big advantage.
- **When do they want to exchange** and complete? They may have a job-related deadline and so be, or not be, in a hurry.
- **Are they a couple who are separating?** This may complicate the selling process as people with possibly different priorities are involved.
- **Is their offer subject to a survey?** Not having another survey will shorten the process.

This information will help you decide what to do. Your estate agent should be able to offer advice here, but remember, although you are paying them, they only get paid if

the property sells, so beware being pushed into selling low just for an early sale.

If the offer is below the asking price, the buyer should give reasons for this, and you can decide if they are valid. Remember your property is only worth what someone is able and prepared to pay for it. Bear in mind also that the market changes and your property might have risen or fallen in desirability in the last couple of months – check this out with your estate agent.

Once you accept an offer, the buyer might ask you to take the house off the market to avoid being gazumped. This is fair enough, but agree a date (for example, in two to six weeks) when you would return to the market if the sale hasn't progressed and/or you have not exchanged. Make sure that they can definitely afford your property and have already accepted an offer or sold their own.

BE CAREFUL!
Whatever the market conditions, communication is crucial. Don't disappear on holiday without telling everybody who needs to know. Respond to emails, letters and phone calls promptly and query anything you don't understand. Agree the timing of regular updates with your estate agent and legal firm.

'Make sure your potential buyer can afford your property.'

Selling in difficult markets

Selling in a falling market

If the price of your property is falling, it is likely to be the same with those that you are looking to buy, and you can actually benefit. For example, if you have to drop £5,000 on your sale price, but negotiate a £10,000 drop on your purchase, you gain £5,000.

- With falling prices there is a risk your buyer may try to renegotiate the price down later on, so agree an early deadline for exchange and completion to give them less time and opportunity.

- Patience is important in a slow market: accept that it will take longer to sell, and watch as more properties fall into your price range.

- The ideal scenario is to sell before buying, perhaps renting somewhere for six months then entering the market as one of those sought-after cash buyers.

Selling in a strong market

You'll know from your research and conversations with estate agents and buyers if the market is buoyant with prices rising and properties selling quickly. You'll benefit from getting a good price on your property, but of course your purchase price may also be high. A rising market is fast moving, which adds to the stress of the whole process and means you need to turn around information quickly – so make sure you have all your paperwork and finances in place.

- Ensure you choose a buyer who is similarly well prepared, and negotiate an early completion date.

- You should aim to buy and sell at the same time in such a market to avoid losing properties of the type you want to buy.

- With demand high it should be easier to sell a property with a drawback, like being on a main road, near a noisy pub or railway, but don't hesitate or try holding out for a higher price: if the market drops, you will be the first casualty.

Problems with your sale

The property selling system varies in different parts of the UK and Ireland, but wherever you are selling (and/or buying) there is enormous potential for problems.

However, you can do a lot to avoid hitches by planning and proceeding sensibly and by taking advice along the way. Your sale is most certainly not as 'safe as houses' – 28 per cent of sales fall through after offer stage, with ramifications in many lives. Here are some ideas of what to do with specific problems.

No viewings

Ask your agent how many sets of particulars of sale they have sent out and why they think no one is viewing the property. Perhaps you need to change some of the photographs or add floorplans, which can be more useful than photographs, because buyers can then see how the property could meet their needs.

Review your marketing strategy. You are either not reaching potential buyers (in which case try different advertising media) or simply not impressing them.

If the particulars of sale are okay, ask yourself if the problem is that your estate agent has a lack of buyers on their lists or is it because it's a terrible market?

Your property doesn't sell

If your property does not sell within eight weeks, there is probably a problem with the valuation or the marketing, which includes the condition your home is in when people view it. If you think it's the latter, look again at pages 114–15. If you're concerned about lack of marketing, you could also try phoning the estate agent pretending to be a potential buyer in the area (or get a friend to do it), and see if they mention your property.

Review your asking price. Have prices dropped locally? What are similar properties selling for? Does your agent think a drop of £5,000 would stimulate new interest?

Continue to bear in mind that clutter and untidiness around the home is not conducive to a quick sale. Look at pages 114-15 to remind you of what makes a home more attractive to a potential buyer.

One criticism levelled at estate agents is that as their commission (see page 93) is a fairly small percentage of the selling price, there is no incentive for them to push for a higher price, but plenty of incentive to get you to accept a lower amount as it makes little difference to the fee they will make. However, they don't get paid until your home sells, so there is still a large incentive.

Bad survey

If your buyer's survey says there are problems with your property, ask for a copy of the relevant parts of the survey. Read it carefully: it may be pointing out potential rather than actual problems that require immediate attention. If you agree a repair is needed, get three estimates. Then you can choose whether to pay to get it done yourself or deduct the money from the sale price. Someone who has got as far as having a survey done has shown they like your property. They won't want to pull out. Incidentally, it is well worth tidying up before the surveyor arrives: part of their job is subjective and a tidy house is more attractive than one where there are piles of washing and toys.

Buyer withdraws

If this happens, you need to find out the reason why. They may have been refused a mortgage and be too embarrassed to tell anyone. However, other lenders may be willing to make them a loan: your

agent or even your financial adviser should have some ideas on this. If they say they've gone off your property, ask why: even if this sale falls through, you're better equipped for the next one.

> **'If you agree that a repair is needed to your home, get hold of three estimates.'**

Your buyer is unable to fund the purchase

This is a quite a common problem but should be avoidable if your estate agent is doing their job properly. Before accepting an offer, ask your agent to check with the purchaser that they have a Mortgage Agreement in Principle in place. If not, keep your property on the market until this is the case.

There can be a problem if the buyer decides to arrange their mortgage through the selling estate agent. This creates a conflict of interest as the agent is making money from both parties in the transaction and cannot therefore act in both their interests. For example, if it emerges that there is a problem with the potential purchaser affording the price they have offered, your estate agent might be tempted to try to lower the price rather than lose the sale and the mortgage arrangement fee. However, this may well happen even if the buyer has the same problem

'The average chain has seven houses. It only takes one sale to run into problems and the whole process grinds to a halt.'

with a separate mortgage company and the agent doesn't want to lose the sale of the property either.

Progress on the sale is very slow

Some buyers seem to view an offer as an 'option to buy' rather than a commitment to purchase, and about one in three purchases fall through. The key here is communication, asking the agent to check that the buyer is serious and has the finances in place before you take your property off the market. The average chain has seven houses. It only takes one sale to run into problems and the whole process grinds to a halt. A good agent will communicate up and down the chain and alert you to any problems.

BE CAREFUL!
Put all instructions and agreements in writing, and send them by registered post so that there can be no dispute on whether they arrived.

Contracts are not exchanging

Talk to your conveyancer and find out what is causing the delay. If you discover the buyer is holding things up or can't raise the finance, set a deadline after which you will put the property back on the market. Don't rely on the ordinary post: use registered post, a courier or deliver things by hand. Find out if there is a delay in another part of the chain and ask your agent or conveyancer to find and solve the problem.

You fall out with your estate agent

If you decide you want to withdraw instructions from your estate agent, inform them by phone first, making a note of the date and time of call and who you spoke to, and telling them you will confirm the conversation in writing. Your contract will tell you what notice period you have to give. Remember that if you instruct another agent during that period and they sell the house, you may still owe commission to your first agent and you could have to pay double. So it makes sense to wait before appointing another agent, although you can still sell privately during this period as long as you didn't sign a contract that contained sole selling rights. Avoid this clause (see also page 100).

If you should hit problems with your sale, see the box Codes of practice on page 99, which contains details of how estate agents are regulated and who you can contact if you need support.

Buying a property

5

The key to buying property is to understand your own needs so that you view places that match your way of life. This chapter discusses the different types of property, including new build, and explains how to check the location will suit you. Then it's on to searching for, viewing and checking out properties: our guidance should save you time and steer you towards the right home for you.

Needs versus wants

Buying a house is a major decision with huge implications for your life and your finances. Try to approach it rationally rather than making it a decision based on what you aspire to. It needs to be right for you at this stage in your life.

Start by assessing what you do want by first choosing the property type that your prefer. When you are briefing an agent, it is all too easy to describe your dream home rather than what you really need and then it can be a big let-down when you find you are not going to be able to have this ideal property. Be as realistic as possible from the outset.

One in three offers falls through and the most common reason is that the buyer finds they can't afford the property that in an ideal world they'd really like. Around 25 per cent of buyers change their mind about what they want once they start looking at properties. That adds up to a lot of wasted time and effort all round. The key is to be realistic, to understand the implications of what you are asking for (every feature comes at a price) and to set an accurate brief that won't lead to frustration and change.

> **'Be as realistic as possible about what you want from the outset.'**

Choosing a property type

Here are three steps to deciding what property type you need and how to achieve it.

Step one

Imagine that you are going to buy a home, and make a list of the features you would look for. For many people, the list may include features such as:
- A double garage.
- A spare room for guests.
- A hot tub.
- An en suite with every bedroom.
- A playroom.
- A study.

This is your wants list.

Step two

Now imagine that you are going to be renting somewhere for a while, and write down what you really need. This list might include the following:
- A bedroom for each child.
- A living area big enough for your furniture.
- A garage or adequate private parking.

- A private, secure garden where your dog can exercise.
- A shared bathroom conveniently situated between two or three bedrooms.
- More storage space.
- Potential to extend.

This is your needs list.

Step three

Now look at what properties in your price bracket have to offer, and how they could be adapted to meet your needs and maybe a few of your wants. For example, a wooden cabin in the garden could function as a study or playroom. You may be able to fit in a bedroom for each child if some of them are single rather than double rooms.

Also consider the implications of the needs and wants list for the type of property you should look at.

- **Basic type:** house, bungalow, flat, mobile home.
- **Kind of house:** detached, semi-detached, terraced.
- **Kind of flat:** ground floor, first or top floor, penthouse, converted or purpose-built.
- **Bedrooms:** how many you need, and how many must be double.
- **Bathrooms/toilets:** how many you need.
- **What other rooms you need:** study, lounge, kitchen/diner, separate dining room.
- **Garden:** small, medium, large, with lawn, general condition.
- **Parking requirements:** off-street, in a garage or carport, for how many cars.

Spare room or hotel suite?

It's lovely to be able to offer guests their own space. But spare rooms are rarely used and often become dumping grounds for possessions on their way somewhere else in the home. If you calculate the extra cost of this largely unused spare room as part of your mortgage, you may find it far cheaper to do without and use the saved cash to book guests into a nearby hotel room as a base for when they come to stay.

Consider different types of property

With your list of needs and wants as a brief, you can now consider which type or types of property are best suited to meet it. Keep your mind open to all possibilities at this stage: you may have pictured yourself living in a Victorian cottage when, in fact, a new-build modern home ticks more of the boxes on your list.

New trends

Private builders are often obliged to include a wider range of properties, including starter homes in 'mixed developments', in return for receiving planning permission. Since 2005 the Government has announced several initiatives to increase the supply of affordable housing, including support for first-time buyers and key workers such as nurses and teachers. Their view is based on: 'A fundamental principle of sustainable communities is that everyone should have the opportunity of a decent home at a price they can afford, in a place in which they want to live and work.' (See also page 139.)

Fashion victim?

Style magazines have a lot to answer for. It's surprising how fashion conscious the property market can be, and people can be led into choosing property styles that just don't suit them. One example is open-plan living/cooking areas. Some buyers realised after a while that they didn't like having cooking smells and sounds competing with the television or the book they were reading. Another example is the industrial-style stainless-steel kitchens, which photograph beautifully but make some people feel as if they are in a factory.

New properties

Buying a new property could allow you to meet many of the requirements on your needs and wants lists. First, developers tend to gear their properties to what the market is demanding, and also, if you get involved early enough, you can influence the planning and layout of your new home. There are a number of benefits to buying new properties (see page 128).

If you opt for a new-build property, do not use a legal firm provided by the developer as there is potential for conflict of interest. Get an independent specialist who is experienced in this area and familiar with issues such as if the property is correctly built on its plot.

Since 2007, lenders have been nervous to lend on some new build properties. As a result, you may have to pay up to a 40 per cent deposit on such a property until lenders have more money for people to borrow and the property market has stabilised. On the other hand, new builds often charge up to 20 per cent price premium over other secondhand homes, apart from character properties. While the property market is in the doldrums, this level of premium isn't always charged, so if you can afford the deposit, new builds can represent increasingly good value for money. Many new builds also have the advantage of offers for first-time buyers, see pages 139–42 for more details.

Jargon buster

Buying off plan When you buy a property that hasn't been built yet, so you are buying it based only on what you can see on the plans.

Listed properties Buildings of historic interest are protected by the 'listing' process, which means owners must seek permission for any changes to the inside or outside of their building. For more information, see page 150.

New build A home that you buy from new or build yourself.

Snagging These are checks for defects after a home has been built, extended or renovated.

 For more information on older properties go to **www.periodproperty.co.uk** and **www.lpoc.co.uk** (the Listed Property Owners Club) where you will find plenty of specialised advice.

Advantages and disadvantages of different styles of property

Age of property	Advantages	Possible drawbacks	Points to note
New homes	■ Little maintenance required for first few years ■ Well-equipped and planned ■ Parking often planned in ■ Well insulated ■ Built to Code level 3 sustainable homes standard	■ Rooms can be small ■ Gardens tend to be small ■ Can lack character ■ Tend to have 'thinner' walls, so not always good sound insulation	■ People often think you don't need a proper survey on a new home, however you do ■ At least cost in a snagging survey or a homebuyer report (see pages 153–4): builders do make mistakes
Post-war homes	■ Use relatively modern construction techniques ■ Tend to be a good size with reasonable gardens ■ Usually built of good quality brick	■ Tend to be on sprawling estates ■ Some of the 1970s homes were built with 'new' materials, which haven't always stood the test of time	■ Can be very good value for money, especially if they are ex-council houses that have now been 'sold' off
1900–1940	■ Usually well built and of reasonable size ■ 1930s homes were some of the first to be built with some building regulations ■ Usually good solid walls with sound insulation ■ Good-sized gardens and driveways for those built after the 1930s ■ Often near to transport links	■ Period features, such as stained-glass windows, can be expensive to maintain/replace ■ Can require a fair amount of maintenance ■ May not have any parking	■ Tend to be good value for money, even within expensive locations ■ Often semi-detached ■ Can feel a little 'estate like'
Pre 1900s	■ Can be very attractive and characterful ■ Original features sometimes still present	■ Layout may not suit lifestyle, e.g. kitchens can be small or there are '2+1' bedrooms – you have to go through one to get to another ■ May require regular maintenance	■ Some may be listed, meaning you need to apply for permission for maintenance and any changes (see page 150) ■ Tend to be more expensive as there is a finite supply

Advantages of buying new properties

Guaranteed purchase

- Once you have agreed the deal, you can exchange quite early on and secure the purchase.
- If you value peace of mind, this is a big plus, but do check the builder can't pull out – prices may have increased since they exchanged and they can then charge more.

Ease of purchase

- The property you are buying will be the end of the chain, so there is less chance of a legal hold-up.
- Some developers will part-exchange your property so you don't have the hassle of selling it (this is a particular attraction in a slow market or if you think your property may be hard to sell).
- Many also offer deals to help you with moving costs.

An easier mortgage

- Some builders fix up mortgage facilities for a development, making it easier to arrange a loan of a high percentage of the price. It won't always be the best deal available.

Extra features

- Fitted kitchens, bathrooms and flooring are often included in the price.

Value for money

- Compared to period properties, new builds can offer a lot for the money.

Design input

- If you buy 'off plan', when the property is at the design stage, you can have a say in the design, layout, fixture and fittings, so it will meet more of your needs and wants.

Decoration

- The property will be freshly decorated, and you may be able to choose colours and styles of decoration if you buy early enough in the build.

Lower upkeep

- New buildings will conform to high standards of insulation, making them energy efficient and less expensive to run.
- Maintenance costs should also be low for the first few years because everything was installed new.

Disadvantages of buying new properties

Faults

- This is a major issue as an average of 80 defects were found in new homes in 2005 even though most had already passed an inspection.
- Nine out of every ten new homes has faults requiring attention.
- Some of these are minor, but they mount up and add to the hassle of moving in: you want a new home, not be part of a building site (see the box on snagging, overleaf).

Price

- You do pay for the extras in the initial price and may have to wait a few years for the price of a new property to move into line with the local market.
- If you have to move sooner, you might not get as much as you paid for it.

Timing

- You may have to wait while the property is finished, and this can be delayed.

Room size

- Some show homes are fitted with smaller-than-average size furniture to make the rooms seem larger.
- Make sure your furniture will fit where you want it.

Garage size

- Single garages can struggle to accommodate some vehicles; check yours will fit.

What will it be like?

- When buying 'off plan' from a brochure it can be hard to picture room proportions, the size of the garden and how close neighbouring properties will be.

Fittings

- There won't be many fittings, such as cupboards and shelves, which are often part of the deal on an existing property.

Living on a building site

- Your home may be finished, but if the rest of the development isn't, you will be living with noise and dirt until the contractors are off site.

Nag about snags

Snagging is the term used for finding the defects after a home has been built. You must have your own independent survey carried out on a new property to identify its faults, and there will be some. Examples include hot and cold taps being swapped, alarms that don't work, uneven floors, poor carpentry, scratched glass or worktops and incomplete damp courses. When you negotiate the contract, ask if you can set an amount or percentage of the price to be held back until all defects are dealt with.

When the faults have been fixed, check again for cosmetic damage and any fresh leaks or problems before approving the work. Your developer is liable for defects discovered during the first two years of your warranty, so report any in writing as soon as you are aware of them. This doesn't cover fair wear and tear. For more information, see www. inspectorhome.co.uk.

Guarantees and insurance

In April 2010, a new Consumer Code to Protect New Build Buyers (www. consumercodeforhomebuilders. com) was introduced to give new home buyers additional protection. This includes buying off plan, recently finished new builds and a renovated property, such as a barn conversion. The code was formed in conjunction with the National House Building Council (NHBC).

'Check what guarantees and insurance come with a new build property. There are several.'

To be protected by this scheme as a buyer, the builder or developer you purchase from needs to be registered with the NHBC and they will deal with any complaints you may have within the first two years of completing your purchase. To date, one case has gone through adjudication and the home owner was repaid £5,000.

New build properties are also protected by a ten-year warranty from the NHBC, Zurich Municipal or Premier Guarantee and Construction Register Ltd, who operate in Northern Ireland, Ireland and Scotland.

The warranties offer protection if the builder goes bankrupt while building the property, for defects that become apparent within two years of completion, and for structural flaws for a further eight years. While this level of protection is helpful, some of the different company guarantees can be fairly weak and the difficulties of having work done after you move in underlines the importance of having an independent survey done, even on newly built properties.

Buying a plot of land and building your own home

With the popularity of property TV programmes such as *Grand Designs* and *Build a New Life in the Country*, many people are gaining confidence in designing their own property either from scratch, or mostly from scratch.

If you are considering finding a property to renovate, convert or buying a plot of land, then be prepared to:

- **Put the time aside you need** – it may literally take years.
- **Move away from where you are now,** unless there is plenty of land around you.
- **Find specialist companies** to work with as the finance, legal element, survey, planning and building regulations, and the price you pay will each require specific knowledge and someone that is used to dealing with 'non-standard' buying and selling.

Searching for land

The first steps are finding the best places to buy land. Try talking to local estate agents and surveyors as they should know the local market and if there are plots available. Grand Designs magazine may have information on local possibilities. There are also website services, such as www.buildstore.co.uk/findingland/, www.selfbuild.co.uk and www.plotfinder.net. However, unlike the free searches from companies such as Rightmove (see page 136) you are likely to have to pay a subscription fee. This can vary tremendously from £20 through to £100 or more a year.

The other problem with these databases is that you don't know how good they are until you subscribe and there are also surprisingly few opportunities available for purchasing land. However, some of the good ones are worth the money, even if you only use them for research purposes. They can help you understand which areas you should start looking in, what sort of prices you are likely to have to pay, and how different areas compare in price. As there is such a shortage of land, some self-builders look to buy a plot with a property they can pull down. As renovating property is increasingly popular, too, many of the finding facilities are adding these to their portfolio. The main things to look out for when choosing databases to work with for finding land are:

- **How up-to-date** the information is (and how it is kept current).
- **Whether the land** included is agricultural (and therefore unlikely to receive planning permission) or already has outlined or even detailed planning permission.
- **Whether the subscription** is lifetime or annual. Lifetime is best due to the time it could take you to find that plot of land.
- **Ability to contact** the company for any help.

 Websites for companies you can contact concerning protection on new homes are: **www.inspectorhome.co.uk**, **www.nhbc.co.uk**, **www.premierguarantee. co.uk**, **www.zurich.co.uk** and, for N. Ireland, **http://structuralinsurance.com/**.

Buying the land

Not all lenders will lend for land, building, converting or renovating property, so you will need to find specialist lenders to help you.

It is worth talking to an independent financial adviser to help you get the best deal or go to a specialist company used to dealing with self-build, conversion and renovation projects.

Fortunately, the days of having to live in a caravan or tent on site are a thing of the past as the market has grown and companies have developed better offerings to help support you. So when you are looking for finance, make sure that:

■ **You have the option** of staying in your home or renting.
■ **They understand** that costs may rise during your project.
■ **They can help** you at every stage of the move.
■ **Depending on your** financial circumstances, they lend the money upfront rather than bit by bit or only after you have purchased your land.

Getting a survey

Make sure that you get a good survey on the land: just because it looks okay to build on, doesn't mean it is. You don't know what's underneath! So do your research

and get specialist surveyors and conveyancers to advise before you buy. Don't forget, too, that you may have to gain planning permission or a view from the local planning department before you purchase too. The planning offices are usually very helpful and local records will tell you if anyone has applied and been rejected or accepted before, so don't be afraid to pick up the phone and chat to them. They may even visit the land/property for you.

Use professionals

When you come to your build, ensure you shop around for services from an architect, project manager or builder. Try to get an independent estimate on what your build might cost. Sometimes you have to pay a few hundred pounds for this, but there are companies that offer this service for free. When it comes to buying your materials, don't be afraid to go to the large merchants – such as Jewson, Wolseley and Travis Perkins – as you may well gain better prices than you would via your builder or project manager. The key message is: shop around or check out the quotes with an independent professional before you agree to them.

Self-build websites to consult include: **www.buildstore.co.uk**; **www.fmb.org. uk**, **www.labc.uk.com** and **www.planningportal.gov.uk**. There are also shows and centres you can visit to find out much more about building or renovation. Check out **www.homebuilding.co.uk**.

Choosing your location

Choosing the right location is sometimes more important than selecting the right style of property, because where you live has a big impact on the lifestyle of everyone in the home.

If the people in your household go out a lot locally, to the shops, pubs, leisure centres or other amenities, they'll want to be able to walk or have an easy drive. An edge of town setting is probably better for you than a home in the middle of the countryside, however idyllic it seems. Similarly, a regular commuter needs to consider the ease of their journey. Is it easy to reach the station? Will your car be crawling across a congested town centre twice a day to get to the main route out? What are the bus routes like?

Traffic is a major issue that can often be overlooked because we tend to view properties at the weekend. Visit the location at different times of the day and on weekdays as well as Sundays. Rush hour can turn the quietest road into a noisy race track. Speed-reducing humps in the road are a telltale sign that it is a rat run for passing traffic. However, there can be other

The highlighter method

When buying a property, buy a street finder map (estate agents often give out local maps) for your target area. Driving or walking around the area will help you identify specific streets or zones that meet your requirements, including the type of property, or areas you just like the 'feel' of. Highlight them on your map so you can quickly spot if new properties on the market are well positioned.

causes: a popular venue for car boot sales could mean there's a queue of vehicles outside your front door on Sunday mornings. Shift patterns in local factories, or being near a school, can cause sudden gluts of traffic - fine if you're always out, but a nuisance if that's when you often start or finish your journeys.

Heavy local traffic is noisy, but there are plenty of other sources of noise: a seemingly peaceful pub might have loud music and an extended licence, which means your road resonates like a disco at

You can research traffic issues by visiting the area at different times of day. Other drawbacks call for different research - see page 148 for matters such as flooding and subsidence.

midnight. It's no fun trying to work or rest at home against a pounding background of heavy machinery from a factory or garage.

New area?

If you are moving to an area you don't know, the best source of information is local people. So visit the area, pop into shops, pubs and information offices, if they have them, and ask, for example, what it's like to live there, which are the best areas, what the crime rate is like. You can ask to be sent copies of the local newspaper (they may make a small charge), and internet searches may well find local community websites, which will give you many insights.

Good estate agents should be able to give you a fair briefing, too. Try the website www.upmystreet.com and the local authority website will often have plenty of information.

Border country

You can get a very good deal if you live close to the border of an area with very good amenities and schools. The property will cost less, the Council Tax is likely to be lower but you will benefit from good services. If choice of school is an important factor in your location, check the catchment area and the policy and availability of places – you can live in a catchment area but still be denied a place if the school or a certain year group is full (see also pages 79–80).

Ask the light questions

The presence of natural light adds to our quality of life and it is important to consider where the property is in relation to the sun. Any room that never gets any sun is likely to feel dark and gloomy, especially in the winter. East-facing rooms get the morning sun (ideal for kitchens), while facing south or west brings some sun for most of the day. So similar houses on opposite sides of a road will feel very different.

Local factors have a big impact on property prices

Prices will be higher near:	Prices will be lowered by proximity to:
■ Highly regarded state schools	■ Noisy pubs and other entertainment venues
■ Good leisure facilities	■ Takeaways with rubbish left close by
■ Convenient shopping	■ Busy roads and flight paths
■ Quality food stores	■ Railway lines
■ Good local transport	■ Waste dumps and derelict land
■ Pleasant countryside and parks	■ Poorly regarded schools
■ Well-maintained private housing	■ Prisons
	■ Masts and pylons
	■ Local authority housing

Finding a property

The traditional way of finding a property is to go through an estate agent. However, this is not the only means – local newspapers and auctions are good alternatives, but there are others, too, which are each described in this section.

Through an estate agent

You can sell your house without an estate agent, but it is unlikely that you will buy without one as more than nine out of ten properties are sold through agencies. The key to getting the best out of an agent is to be prepared and to be as straightforward as possible.

Before seriously briefing an agent on what you want, get your finances in place, including your Mortgage Agreement in Principle (MAP) (see pages 40–1), and prepare your brief of what you really need. Look for agents who sell the types of property you want – check websites and local newspaper advertisements (see also pages 84–5).

A good agent will ask for information that will tell them how serious you are about buying. This will influence the level of service you get, because you don't pay them and they'll only want to put in effort that might result in a sale. Be honest: estate agents don't have the best reputation for honesty, but most can provide a long list of lies they've been told at this stage.

They'll want to know the following particulars:

- **Is your property on the market?** How close are you to a sale?
- **Have you got a MAP** or are you a cash buyer?
- **What are you looking for?**
- **How much can you afford?**

As discussed already, your brief should not describe your ideal home, but be a wide list of the types of property, locations and features that you are looking for, together with the reasons. For example, explain that you need a big garden for your dog, or a double bedroom because your children like to share their room. Print a copy for them to keep. The most common mistake

'The key to getting the best out of an estate agent is to be organised, prepared and to be straightforward.'

'Putting the word about that you are interested in buying could lead to a sale without the property even reaching the market.'

Other ways of finding a property

There are alternatives to estate agents, and most people start their search on the internet where there are agents' and private sale sites (see box, top right). This is a good way to start getting a 'feel' for the market. In addition, there are several other routes that might lead to a private sale.

Local newspapers

Sellers marketing their own property are likely to advertise in the local property newspapers or publications such as Loot. Papers will send copies to your address if you don't live locally – there may be a small fee for this. Or many will have their own websites.

people make is to rush into briefing an agent on their perfect home, then start backtracking later when they realise their needs are different, or they can't fund it.

The agent will supply you with details of properties within about 10 per cent of your price range. You can probably download details from their internet site, but also call each week to check if anything has just come on the market and not been through the system yet.

If you make an appointment for a viewing and can't make it, tell the agent. They'll appreciate you not wasting their time and being able to keep the seller informed. If a property suitable for you suddenly comes on the market and they need a quick sale, they're more likely to contact you if you are well organised and flexible than if they come to see you as a time-waster.

Private and specialist internet property sites

www.eigroup.co.uk
www.findaproperty.com
www.houseweb.co.uk
www.primelocation.com
www.propertybroker.co.uk
www.rightmove.co.uk
www.ruralscene.co.uk
www.ruralpropertyindex.co.uk
www.periodproperty.co.uk
www.zoopla.co.uk

To find local papers in an area, check the website **www.newspapersoc.org.uk** (the Newspaper Society), which allows you to search for daily and weekly local papers, both paid for and free.

Your own contacts

Everyone has a network of friends, contacts and relatives. Putting the word about that you are interested in buying could possibly lead to a private sale.

Employers

Many firms have noticeboards and you may be able to advertise your interest in local property. Large companies have human resources departments who will be aware of anyone leaving, or perhaps relocating within the firm to another site. It costs little to ask for this information and you could strike it lucky. It's possible that the company has agreed to sell their employee's home as part of a relocation package, in which case they'll be delighted to hear from you.

Notes through doors

This can be very productive. Everyone likes being complimented on their home, and a polite note put through the door saying how much you love it and if they would tell you if and when they'd like to sell might prompt someone into offering you a property. This is particularly worth trying when there is a shortage of your preferred property type.

Auctions

Auctions are undoubtedly a source of some cheap property, but you have to know what you are doing, because you have to spend money up front on a survey and legal checks before even bidding. Some 30,000 properties are sold by auction each year (just under 2 per cent of the market) – some homes may have been repossessed, some where the owner died without a will, and standard homes or properties that are likely to attract very little or a great deal of interest. You must get a survey on any property you buy through auction – before you bid.

You have to hand over 10 per cent of your successful bid on the day and pay the balance within 28 days. You can offer bids in advance and if the property is listed as 'unless previously sold', the seller may take your offer to save the trouble and expense of the auction process. Don't go down the auction route unless you definitely have the cash – including the full backing of any lender. Set a bidding limit of what you can afford and don't exceed it – if you're worried about getting carried away in the excitement, get someone you trust to do the bidding for you.

Websites giving auction details include **www.eigroup.co.uk**. *Property Auction News* magazine covers this field, too. For more information, go to: **www.propertyauctionnews.co.uk**.

> **'Talk to property developers who are offering part-exchange deals to encourage buyers for their estate.'**

Discounted property

Getting property at a discount is a full-time job for an expert unless you are very lucky. The first step is to know the local market inside out, so that you know the genuine value of the property types and locations in which you are interested. Experts suggest that about one in every 150 properties they view turns out to be a bargain – and they will already have vetted many from the particulars.

All the non-agent methods listed on pages 136–7 should offer some kind of discount because the seller is not paying commission to an agent. Indeed, auction properties

are more than a third cheaper than similar ones bought through high street agencies.

But not everyone is willing or able to wait for the right property to come up at auction and risk money on what could be a wasted survey. By keeping in contact with estate agents you stand a good chance of hearing about a reduction due to a seller needing to move quickly because of changing circumstances. Other reasons for discounted sales are as follows:

- **Repossessions,** when the loan company takes over a property and will want to get rid of it quickly.
- **Relocations,** when someone needs to move to a new job. Large firms that offer relocation packages to senior staff are prepared to sell fast.
- **A chain collapsing** and a seller needing a new buyer quickly to ensure their own purchase goes through. This can be caused by a buyer dying, separating from a partner or hitting financial problems. In such circumstances you become the hero who saves the day.

Another route is to talk to property developers who are offering part-exchange deals to encourage buyers for their estate. They will be keen to sell the homes their buyers have left as quickly as possible, and that may mean the price is right for you.

Front of the grid

You can put yourself in a position to take advantage of any good deals that become available by selling your property and renting until the right home comes up at a good price. You can then put yourself on the front of the starting grid by making an offer as a cash buyer. However, there are increased costs involved, so make sure it's worth your while.

First-time buyer schemes

The media often make out that it's impossible for buyers to get on the ladder, claiming you need tens of thousands of pounds for a deposit and quoting average ages of 37 or even 43 years before you can buy.

These figures aren't always accurate and in reality you may well be able to afford a property locally. If prices are too high, you may have access to special first-time buyer schemes that require less than £5,000 for a deposit or give support to buy a home if you are a social tenant.

First-time buyer affordability

Since November 2011, the Government has released some new schemes and enhanced some old ones to try to help first-time buyers and people living in social housing get onto the property ladder. For first time buyers, the help is via buying new-build properties, and for social tenants, it is typically substantial help to purchase the home lived in for some time.

All the schemes have different eligibility criteria, so it's important to contact the right organisations and people so you don't end up going down a route that you later find doesn't work for you. It is also important to bear in mind that the rules, eligibility and schemes change over time and can be different for Scotland, England, Wales and Northern Ireland. Here we concentrate on looking at schemes available in England and Wales.

First-time buyer schemes

For people who don't live in social housing, there are three ways in which you can secure help to afford a home of your own. They all relate to buying a new build that hasn't yet been lived in by someone else and you can be eligible even if you have joint incomes of up to £60,000. The first scheme is NewBuy, the second shared equity, and the third shared ownership. Whichever scheme you are interested in, it is worth contacting a HomeBuy

→ For schemes that are available in Scotland, Northern Ireland and Ireland, see pages 194, 197 and 202-3.

HomeBuy contacts

The Homes & Communities Agency supports a scheme called HomeBuy. If you want to find out if you are eligible for any HomeBuy schemes, contact a HomeBuy Agent. These are the Government's appointed one-stop shops for applications and information and you can find out more from www.homebuy.co.uk.

Agent as they will help you find out what schemes you are eligible for and save you time going from one housing association or developer site to another (see the HomeBuy contacts box, above).

NewBuy

This is a scheme to help first-time buyers who can afford the mortgage on a property but are struggling to purchase a property as they can't afford to save for the deposit. The scheme is backed by the Government and is actually a support to lenders who offer mortgages requiring just a 5 per cent deposit to first-time buyers (and other people struggling locally). If the property price falls over time and the buyer ends up being forced to sell and is in negative equity, the Government has guaranteed the lender offering the deal to fund any shortfall. For more information visit www.newbuy.org.uk.

Shared equity

This scheme is for selected new build properties to enable them to be bought direct from the developer with a top-up loan. Buyers need to be able to afford at least 70 per cent of the property's value and this is funded via a deposit and a conventional mortgage. The other 30 per cent funding is purchased with an additional loan, which is fee free for the first five (or more) years of ownership.

For example, if a property was worth £125,000 and you buy 70 per cent of the property you would pay £87,500 for the property. If you are then putting down a deposit of 10 per cent, which would be £8,750, you would then secure a mortgage for the rest – £78,750. The advantage is that you live in the whole property but don't have to pay for the rest of it for the first five or more years or when you come to sell the property.

Shared ownership

This is a different way of owning a home and is increasingly popular in areas across the UK. The scheme is offered by local authorities and housing associations and allows people to live in a home outright, but only purchase a percentage of a new home and pay rent on the rest. With shared ownership, people typically buy a minimum of 25 per cent of the property, but can buy 50 or 75 per cent. Over time, as income grows, people can either remain with just a share of the property or buy the property outright.

For example, if you purchase 25 per cent of a property worth £150,000, you will need to fund

£37,500 of which a 10 per cent deposit will be just £3,750.

The advantage of this scheme is that although you have the use of the whole property, you share the risk of any property price falls with the owner. If you own more than 25 per cent of the property and hit hard times, it may also be possible to reduce your shareholding to make your home more affordable. Bear in mind, though, that you will be responsible for 100 per cent of the property's maintenance (unless it's a flat).

Can your family help?

If you have enough money for the deposit, but need to borrow more than your income multiple allows on a mortgage, your parents can help by acting as a guarantor, which means you could secure a mortgage. But if you default, they will be pursued for the debt by your lender.

If you are short on the deposit, extra cash from parents as a gift or loan can help. If you are planning to do this, seek some independent financial help, especially with regard to Inheritance Tax so that the money is loaned in the best way for all parties and, if required, declared to the lender.

If your parents haven't the cash to help, they could re-mortgage their own property; however, they

---

Jargon buster

Key worker living A scheme that aims to help NHS staff, teachers, police officers, prison and probation staff, and social workers to buy a home in London, the south east and east of England.

Shared equity This is where you purchase a percentage of the property and can wait five or more years before you buy the rest of the property.

Shared ownership A way in which you buy a share of the property and pay rent on the rest.

---

would incur costs to remortgage and would have to pay more money for their own mortgage every month, so it is best to seek legal and financial advice and even have an agreement drawn up.

Finally, if you are buying with a partner, make sure that an agreement is drawn up as to what happens with regards to your parents' financial help – if you fall out, they could walk away with your parents' hard-earned cash!

Buying with others

Pooling your resources with one or more friends or relatives could help. Many lenders won't consider more than two people for a mortgage together, although it is possible for up to four people to jointly own a property. If you are to be joint owners, you'll need a legal agreement establishing how ownership is

---

Housing advice and housing association websites include:
www.direct.gov.uk; **www.housinginwales.co.uk**; **www.icsh.ie**; **www.nifha.org**; **www.sfha.co.uk** and **http://england.shelter.org.uk**.

shared. This is crucial because at some stage one of you is likely to want to leave. The options are:

- **Joint tenants** have equal rights to the whole property and if one dies, the other inherits it, irrespective of the will of the deceased.
- **Tenants in common:** each have a specific (not necessarily equal) share in the property, which, in the event of one dying, will go to whoever is named in their will.

If you have a joint mortgage, you will both be responsible for the monthly payments, even if one of you leaves – so one person can be saddled with the whole mortgage, or perhaps worse, has to sell their property. None of the joint owners can be forced to leave, and the property can only be sold with agreement of them all. They should make a legal agreement about how to split the proceeds as otherwise they could end up in court.

Sharing the cost of buying might seem a good idea, but can turn into a nightmare, so agree in writing, in advance, what you would do if either of you wants/needs to sell up. The agreement should include how to value the property, each share and notice required to leave or sell.

Buying to let a room

To help you afford your first mortgage, if you can buy a property with a spare room or two, you could rent out one of the rooms and earn up to £4,250 per year – tax free. There are some mortgages that are available on this basis. You need to compare the extra mortgage costs with the additional rent you would secure and any tax you may owe from rent.

Off to the park

A growing trend in the UK property market is for elderly people to buy a park home. This is either a permanent construction, usually a bungalow, or a large static caravan, located in a private park setting. In 2002, more than 120,000 people were living in park homes in England and Wales alone, and the figure is rising.

Park homes attract those who wish to downsize to a smaller property and to whom the private, rural setting appeals. Typical sizes of these homes are around 11 x 4m (35 x 12ft), giving a larger living space than many flats. There are often age restrictions, and many parks do not accept resident children or pets.

Park home information sites include **www.communities.gov.uk**; **www.iphas. co.uk**; **www.theparkhome.net** and **www.ukparks.com**. Some offer more specialised information than others, but it's worth taking a look at them all.

Viewing property

Just as you probably have an emotional link with your own home, so the heart can rule the head when viewing. It can also be tricky wandering around an unfamiliar property with a stranger, whether it is with an agent or the owner.

Viewing is easier with someone else to share impressions with, and to interact with the guide if you find it difficult. If a property meets your needs but the particulars don't appeal, view it anyway – it might turn out to be your dream home.

You do need to consider the ambience of the place and whether it could ever feel like home, but there are practicalities to consider, too. Take a printout of your 'needs' list and tick off or add a comment against each one as you explore the property.

A checklist for viewing

Use this checklist to act as prompts for what to look at when viewing a property.

Outside	Look for
Front – garden, entrance	▪ Tidiness, cracked or broken surface
Roof	▪ Missing tiles
Brickwork	▪ Wear, cracks, bulges
Chimneys	▪ Crookedness, damp bottom bricks
Drains and gutters	▪ Leaks and cracks
Window frames	▪ Paintwork, signs of rot

Inside, by room	Look for
Decoration	▪ Quality and condition (can you live with it for a while?)
Power sockets	▪ Number and location, age of electrical system
TV point	▪ Location
Storage	▪ Is there enough, or potential for it?
Flooring	▪ Quality and condition (does any need replacing?)
Evidence of damp	▪ Condensation, mould, fresh paint (see box, overleaf)
Central heating	▪ Age of boiler and age/condition of radiators
Room size/layout	▪ Possibilities for knocking through

'If the property has been on the market for more than 12–16 weeks, it suggests there could be a problem with selling it.'

It is especially important to consider the layout. For example, some Victorian properties have a third bedroom, which can only be reached through another room, which can be very inconvenient.

Try to ignore the décor: it is the easiest thing to change if you don't like it. If it is not to your taste, it could put you off an otherwise suitable property. Bear in mind the points given in the checklist for viewing on page 143.

Don't be wet

Water damages buildings so when you are viewing a property, look for signs of damp such as its distinctive smell, plaster coming off the walls, and if any wallpaper or paint is peeling. Damp can be disguised by special paint, so be suspicious of any patches of fresh paint, especially if they are in corners and on ceilings.

Some practicalities

Be as 'hands on' as you can:

- **Run the hot tap** to see how long it takes for hot water to arrive. In new houses, check the hot and cold taps are correctly fitted.
- **Check that the light switches** work.
- **Where is the boiler** and when was it last serviced? Have the sellers got the paperwork to prove it?
- **Where is the fuse box** and when was it last checked?
- **Where is the water stopcock?** Is the water metered?
- **Do the windows** open and shut properly?

Also see overleaf for questions to ask the vendor or agent who takes you around the property. After you have finished viewing any property, keep the details, including your notes. This can help you make comparisons and could be useful if, for example, a property that has been sold after you viewed it unexpectedly returns onto the market.

Such a file is also useful when speaking with agents as you can give the addresses of properties you do or don't like – it will help them gauge what might interest you.

 It is only when you have decided on which property you would like to pursue that you need to start concerning yourself with more detailed information such as flooding and subsidence – see pages 147–51.

What to ask the vendor or agent

Ask the right questions and you will learn a lot more about the property than by just looking around it.

'How long has the property been on the market?'

Anything more than 12 weeks suggests there could be a problem with selling the property. For example, it may be overpriced.

'How many people have viewed it?'

Again, a high number of viewings with no offer suggests that the property isn't being viewed by the right people, or that there may be an issue with the property.

'Have any offers been made and/or accepted?'

This will tell you the degree of genuine interest. A lack of offers or ones that fall through suggest the property might be overpriced or faulty. Bear in mind it is illegal for an agent to tell you how much someone else offered on the property.

'Have any sales fallen through? Why?'

There are many reasons a sale could have collapsed. If it was clearly the buyer changing their mind or not having the finance ready (both very common), that need not reflect on the property. If they pulled out for unspecified reasons, be alert for why this might have been.

'Has the vendor got a property to move to?'

This will help inform you how serious the vendor is – people do change their minds. A vendor keen to move to a property they have offered on might be prepared to drop the price.

'Why is the vendor moving?'

Most people move as they are expanding or decreasing the family size, or moving in together for the first time. However, sometimes people move due to problems with neighbours or noise. Buying from vendors who are separating can slow the process as they might not be communicating or in agreement.

'What is included in the price?'

This is important as there may be fixtures and fittings you don't want (and therefore don't want to pay for) or do want but they are not part of the deal.

'Would the vendor negotiate on the price?'

A good agent will have discussed a minimum price the vendor might accept, so it is worth asking the agent who is selling the property as you may be given a steer.

'Can I see the EPC?'

This gives you an idea of utility bill costs. See pages 105-7.

When do you know it's the right one?

Some people comment that they 'just fell in love with' the house they bought. There is certainly a place for gut feeling, but this is a big, expensive decision and it pays to be rational, too. Don't commit yourself to the first property you view: compare it with at least another five as it will help you decide if the one you like represents value for money. Arrange a second viewing, preferably at a different time and on a different day (so you can see how the light is different and what traffic and noise levels are like then). Take along your most sceptical friend who can be relied on to make challenging observations.

Go over the advice on location on pages 133–4 and try to check traffic and noise conditions at different

The square metre test

The square metre test helps you decide if a house is good value for money. Calculate the total square metres of the property from the layout or from the room dimensions (the property's size in square metres should be on the EPC), and divide it into the asking price (see page 88). This will give you a cost per square metre. Do the same with other properties you viewed or have details of so that you can make a comparison. This is useful as it is completely objective and helps to show how much space you are getting for your money.

times of the day. If you don't do this then you could get a nasty shock when you move in and discover that traffic jams form outside your home twice a day, meaning you can't get out or park on your return, or noisy neighbours regularly have parties at night.

Find more detail on the property (see below) and when you are really confident you've found somewhere that meets your 'needs' requirements (and maybe a few 'wants'), is in a suitable location and offers good value for money, you should make some more specific checks.

> 'Try to check traffic and noise conditions at different times of day – otherwise you could get a nasty shock when you move in and discover traffic jams forming outside your home twice a day.'

Find more detail on a property you are interested in, including the price it sold for last time, by looking at websites such as **www.findaproperty.co.uk** and **www.mouseprice.com** or for £4 at **www.landreg.gov.uk**.

Checking out a property

However much you like a property and are tempted to make an offer, it makes sense to make a few basic checks first. This saves time in the long term because it will alert you to any problems that may put you off the purchase altogether.

Making checks will also help you to make an offer that reflects the value of the property.

When most buyers look at a property, their decision is based on whether the property feels like 'home' and is somewhere they can envisage living in for the next few years, or indeed as long as they can.

One thing that many people forget, though, is that when you buy a home, what you are actually buying is a building that has been built on a piece of land. In the UK, over 60 per cent of properties were built before 1965, so are already over 40 years old, and 35 per cent of properties were built before the Second World War, so are over 60 years old.

Properties are not all built in the same way, for example properties pre-1930 typically don't have strong foundations like new ones have today. Work may also have been made to the property prior

to stricter checks, so even if a boiler or the electrics have recently been modernised, they haven't necessarily been carried out to the standards required today.

It's not just the building that needs to be checked. We have also started to see the effects that changes in climate, such as less rain, can have. A heavy clay soil, for example, can contract when the weather is very

CON29DW

This is a specialist search you need ensure has been carried out by your solicitor/conveyancer. Basically it checks what water and sewerage services are provided to your property. The Con29DW legally protects you from any errors in the search, which if made, could cost thousands to fix. Visit www.con29drainagewater.co.uk for more information.

 These websites will give you some idea of the value of similar properties in your area: **www.nethouseprices.com** and **www.rightmove.co.uk**. See also the box on page 136.

dry, causing cracks to appear in properties built on the clay. These cracks may or may not be an issue, but will always need investigating. Conversely, more rain may, of course, mean that a property that had previously never been flooded may now be part of a flood plain.

Before you make that offer, it is therefore essential to have the building (your home!) thoroughly checked for any problems and know more about the environment your property has been built in.

The three biggest risks to property are flooding, subsidence and radon.

Flooding

It can take a year to renovate a property after a serious flood, never mind the emotional and physical trauma you will suffer. Sea encroachment and coastal erosion threaten 1.5 per cent of the country, while 7 per cent of the country is likely to flood at least once every 100 years when rivers burst their banks, and many more properties

> '**Around 5 million people, in 2 million properties, live in flood risk areas in England and Wales.**'

Policy decision

If the property you are purchasing is at risk from environmental factors and you are concerned about getting insurance, ask the owner what policies they have and who they are with. You may be able to continue cover in the same way with the same firm.

could suffer from flash floods. Around 5 million people, in 2 million properties, live in flood risk areas in England and Wales.

In addition to the risk of water invasion, such properties are more expensive to insure. Visit www.environment-agency.gov. uk for information on flood risk by postcode area. You can also contact www.homecheck.co.uk for a free summary risk report or gain a more comprehensive assessment, including other risks, such as contamination, radon and subsidence (charges from £11.50, although your legal firm might do this as part of their search).

Subsidence

This is when a property has moved because the ground beneath it can no longer support it. It can be caused by building over old mineshafts, tree roots growing into foundations, or long-term drought

---

You can get information from the Health Protection Agency radon hotline on 01235 822622 (**www.hpa.org.uk**) and **www.environment-agency.gov.uk** and **www.homecheck.co.uk**.

drying out the soil. Subsidence is a rare, but serious problem and should be picked up in your survey as it creates large cracks in the walls.

Radon

Radon is a natural radioactive gas that is thought to represent a cancer risk when inhaled in large quantities. Good ventilation in houses can stop radon gas building up and there is a simple test kit to assess build-up. New homes in high-risk areas (which are mainly but not exclusively in the southwest of England and west Wales) must meet building regulations designed to protect against radon build-up. For further information, see box, opposite below.

Checks and guarantees

Legislation introduced in January 2005 states that any but the most basic electrical work must be carried out by a competent person, who must provide a certificate of safety. To understand what you can and can't do in a property, visit the new rules for electrical safety in the home at www.planningportal. gov.uk/uploads/br/BR_PDF_PTP_ NEWRULES english.pdf.

For your own peace of mind, always get the gas and electrics checked once your offer has been

accepted. Go to a specialist service that will check both. The electrical check should cost from £100, with the gas check from £55, depending on the area you live in. Go to a local company or www.gas-elec. co.uk for more information.

Also ask which guarantees are valid on the property relating to any of the following: damp, timber treatment, the boiler, flooring and carpets.

Check if the company that provided the service is still trading, otherwise the guarantee may have no value. A good timber or damp treatment firm will give you a free estimate and details of work that needs to be done.

Keep your guarantees

If you buy the property, keep all paperwork relating to these checks and guarantees in a 'house' file. Keeping this information will be valuable if you choose to sell the property in the future. If you don't keep it, and can't prove work or services are guaranteed, you could have to spend a lot of money having it done again. This is especially the case for the energy performance certificate.

Listed properties

Listed buildings are deemed to be of architectural or historical interest and are protected by law from significant change. There are

---

For information on gas and electricity checks, see **www.communities.gov.uk**, **www.niceic.org.uk** (the National Inspection Council for Electrical Installation Contracting) and **www.eca.co.uk** (the Electrical Contractors' Association).

three levels of listing, from Grade I (exceptional interest), to Grade II (more than special interest – most listed residential properties fall into this category) to Grade III (of special interest, worth preserving). There are about 370,000 such properties in England and Wales, they are usually over 150 years old and form a valued part of the landscape. Owners of listed buildings cannot make changes that would alter the character of the property (inside or out) without obtaining permission from the local planning authority. These are unlikely to sanction altering the windows, installing new fireplaces or replacing internal walls, and may decide against other changes, such as fitting burglar alarms, TV dishes or aerials.

Listed buildings are likely to be highly attractive and tend to be sold at premium prices. They can be expensive to run as working on them requires specialist craftsmen. There is no difference in how they are bought or sold, but it is important to check the grade of listing and whether it applies to all or part of the property. You should choose surveyors and legal firms with experience of such buildings.

Some localities known as conservation areas also have regulations banning anything changing their character, which can extend to refusal to allow trees to be cut down.

Buying a flat

Flats and apartments are attractive purchases for anyone who wants to live near the buzz of a city centre or to whom 'loft-style living' appeals. Developers have converted old buildings into blocks of apartments, some of which have shared leisure facilities. Such properties appeal to those people who don't need lots of living space: those without children, and downsizers.

Buying a flat is more complicated than buying a house because someone else owns the rest of the building and the land it stands on. The owner is known as the freeholder, and the purchaser of the flat is the leaseholder for a specified period. Their responsibilities typically break down as shown in the box opposite.

When considering purchasing a flat, it is important to experience what noise levels are like between the properties (some are much better insulated than others) and to talk to fellow residents to discover how well people get on and how matters such as routine maintenance are handled.

Websites that have all sorts of different information about listed properties include: **www.english-heritage.org.uk**, **www.heritage.co.uk**, **www.periodproperty.co.uk** and **www.lpoc.co.uk** (the Listed Property Owners Club).

The legal aspect of buying a flat tends to take an extra couple of weeks and be more expensive (from £100 extra) because there is more paperwork and there are more checks to do. Key questions to ask include the following:

■ How are major one-off costs such as replacing the roof or windows covered?

■ What are the service charges, what do they cover and are they likely to rise?

■ How do I contact the freeholder or managing agent?

Always read the leasehold agreement carefully and watch out for restrictions on things such as sub-letting a room, keeping pets, noise and where you can hang up your washing. Ask your conveyancer for a summary of key restrictions just in case you missed something.

Also find out early on how long the lease has to run. You may have trouble getting a loan if it is less than 80 years, in which case you may want to investigate whether the freeholder would extend it. This is often a source of conflict between the two parties.

Costs of renewing a lease

If you are buying a property with a lease of 85 years or less, it is worth finding out about the costs and ease (or not) of renewing the lease. Many lenders won't lend on a property that has fewer than 80 years left on the lease, restricting the market you can sell to and potentially impacting on the property's value. For more information about renewing a lease, contact the Association of Leasehold and Enfranchisement Practitioners at www.alep.org.uk.

Freeholder and leaseholder responsibilities	
	Responsible for
Freeholder	■ Buildings insurance ■ Maintenance and repairs of the property's communal areas such as the roof and stairways
Leaseholder	■ Ground rent ■ Service charges ■ Contents insurance ■ Costs of upkeep shared with other leaseholders

Making your offer

Some people find the negotiation stage exciting, others hate it. Try to distance yourself from your emotions and treat it as a business transaction – how would you behave if it was part of your normal job?

Many factors will influence how much you decide to offer for the property, including:

- **Local market conditions:** are they stable, rising or falling?
- **How long** it's been on the market.
- **Prices of similar properties.**
- **How many of your needs** the property meets.
- **How much** you like it.
- **The price** per square metre.
- **The 'fit'** you have with the vendor in terms of when you'd want to move.
- **If you are a cash or first-time buyer,** you are in a stronger position than someone with a property to sell.

Your offer will be subject to the survey and contract, so you are not legally committing yourself to this price. Given this, and knowing what you can afford, you might offer the asking price or a figure below it. When you make this offer to the agent explain your rationale: what is your evidence that it is worth less than the asking price? What flaws or concerns have influenced you? You might want to make your offer subject to certain conditions apart from the survey. For example, there may be a flaw you need reassurance on. In particular, you can set a deadline on when you will exchange and complete. Make these conditions explicit and in writing.

The agent is legally obliged to pass on your offer to the vendor in writing. Ask for a copy to ensure it happens and is accurate. If you offer below the asking price, expect to negotiate. Don't be offended if the seller simply rejects the bid. Go over your sums again and if you are sure you are right with the value, tell the agent you'd like to look at other properties. A good agent will be able to judge whether to advise the seller to negotiate or not.

The common scenario if there is not a vast gap between the asking and offer prices is to eventually split the difference. So if the seller wanted £200,000 and you offered £188,000, you might both be prepared to settle at £194,000. The sums of money are enormous and you must be sure you are happy with the price, because now you're going to be spending your own, non-refundable money to check out the purchase.

Getting a survey

The condition of a property affects its price. If you buy one in poor condition, you may get it below market price, but it may have already been adjusted down to take into account the money needing to be spent on it. Know what is required.

In Scotland it is now a requirement for a seller to produce a Home Report that includes information about a property's condition and a valuation for mortgage purposes. However, for everywhere else in the UK it is the buyer's responsibility to get the property properly checked for physical problems that could affect its value.

Surveys

There was, and continues to be, much confusion over surveys. Many buyers mistake the mortgage valuation their lender prepares for a survey. In actual fact, the mortgage valuation is just a check that the property exists and is worth more than they are loaning. If that valuation is at odds with what you have offered, you may not be able to go ahead with the purchase. The lender may also set certain conditions, such as completion of a damp course, before agreeing the loan.

Unfortunately you have to pay for the lender's mortgage valuation – and it can cost around £300. You must also commission your own

---

Jargon buster

Buildings survey Also called a structural survey, this provides a detailed report on the property's construction.
Condition report This complements a mortgage valuation to assess the property's overall condition.
Homebuyer report A standard report that evaluates any urgent repairs.
Mortgage valuation A report commissioned by your lender to check the property is valued correctly.

'A seller has to produce a Home Report in Scotland. It should include information about the property's condition and also a valuation for mortgage purposes.'

independent survey, even if the property is newly built. The good news is that surveys often identify faults that allow you to negotiate the price, so they often pay for themselves. You now have a choice of four types: **condition report**, **homebuyer report**, **buildings survey** and **snagging survey**.

Condition report

This report gives a general assessment of a property's condition, but doesn't include a valuation. A condition report is provided by the Royal Institution of Chartered Surveyors (RICS) and by a Home Inspector from www.rpsa. org.uk. It can be used by sellers to find out if there are any key issues with their property or for buyers who don't need a homebuyer report or building survey.

> '**There are four types of survey a buyer can choose from: Condition report Homebuyer report Buildings survey Snagging survey.**'

Homebuyer report

This is suitable for most post-1930s properties of standard construction that do not seem to have any structural problems. It covers the general condition of the property, including the following features.

- Roof, chimney, tiles and flashing.
- Walls, floors and ceilings.
- Guttering and drainage.
- Windows and doors.
- Structure and build quality.
- Location and surrounding area.

You should investigate any problems highlighted by the easy to follow colour coded condition ratings. It will usually be easier and cheaper to get the relevant specialist firm to advise on this, rather than employ a surveyor. You will not be able to employ the same surveyor who may have produced the home condition report because of the potential conflict of interest. However, if there are structural problems, you may need to commission a building or structural survey.

A homebuyer report takes several hours to complete and the average cost is £500. Try to accompany the surveyor as you are bound to learn about the property.

If you have noticed anything about the property, such as signs of damp, or bulges in plaster or brickwork, brief your surveyor on this.

 To find out more about different types of surveys, visit **www.rics.org** and **www.rpsa.org.uk/**. For Northern Ireland, visit **www.rics.org/northernireland** and for Ireland, go to **www.scsi.ie/Surveys**. See also **www.newhomeadvisor.co.uk**.

Buying in difficult markets

Buying in a falling market

When prices start falling, you may feel that you could be paying too much for a property that will be worth less in three months' time. This may be the case, but remember why you are buying it (presumably because you really want to live there) and that in the long-term, prices have historically risen.

- Bear in mind that if you wait for prices to fall further, your own sale price could drop too.

- If you can, sell up and rent or stay with friends for a while so that you can keep looking and go in as a cash buyer.

- Expect to negotiate the price down, explaining your understanding that prices generally are dropping.

Buying in a strong market

There are additional pressures when buying in a strong market: you can feel as if this is your last chance to jump on or up the property ladder before it gets yanked out of reach. When properties are selling fast and prices are rising, you need to be well organised and prepared.

- Be sure you have your finances in place and have a clear, wide brief for the agent.

- Process paperwork fast.

- Check that your vendor has a property to move to, or ask if they are prepared to move out and rent or stay with friends to complete the sale quickly.

- Be careful not to choose an unsuitable property under pressure of rising prices: it will be hard to sell next time around.

Buildings survey

This is a more thorough assessment suitable for older properties or anything of non-standard construction.

- It goes into more detail, for example, on the condition of the timber and pests.
- It involves more work than the homebuyer report, and so will cost more (from £500 upwards).

When you receive the report, read it carefully. Surveys often recommend specialist inspections of particular problems. Always follow these up. Tradesmen will give you a more accurate estimate free of charge, and you can get timber and damp surveys for free from firms specialising in their treatment. A sensible vendor will have obtained estimates on the work required to fix the problem, and you may be able to negotiate on who will pay, or a reduction in the sale price.

Check that any boundary fences or walls match the Land Registry map. It might not, especially on new and renovated property.

Snagging survey

This is a specific survey for new builds. Although new builds come with either a National House Building Council, Zurich, Premier Guarantee or Construction Register guarantee, they only take into account the structure of the property. However, they do identify common issues such as ill-fitting sockets and poor plumbing. Snagging surveys can cost from under £200 to £500 (there is a higher charge if they negotiate with the developer on your behalf).

'When you receive a report, read it carefully. Surveys often recommend specialist inspections for particular problems. You should always follow these up.'

Managing the chain

6

Property chains can be the stuff of nightmares: so many people's lives can be adversely affected by one person's actions. This chapter explains how to find out what is happening up and down the chain and what you can do to keep things moving so that you get into your new home on schedule.

Running the chain gang

The chain is the series of buyers and sellers linked together because each is selling and purchasing a property from one of the others, apart from the people at either end.

Property chains can put people off buying property, creating such a series of delays, confusion, stress and worry that many people swear 'Never again!' … but often later find that they must go through it all once more.

Part of the problem is the number of people involved, none of them with a bird's eye view of the whole process. A typical chain in England or Wales features seven properties, each with at least one seller, plus their estate agent, legal firm, surveyor, lender, and other service providers. There could easily be 50 people involved, each with a crucial role at some point, and if one of them forgets to sign a piece of paper, loses a document, misses a phone message, neglects to check a detail, accidentally deletes all their emails, or disappears on holiday, the whole chain could be delayed. The impact of this on the buyers' and sellers' lives can be enormous. Added to this is the problem that property deals seem to bring out the worst in people: they can get very greedy and selfish, at a massive cost to others.

A property chain could form like this particular example:

- **A:** First-time buyer, purchasing a bedsit from …
- **B:** … a single woman trading up to a two-bedroom house owned by …
- **C:** … a couple moving to a three-bedroom house with room for their two young children. They are buying from …
- **D:** … a professional couple with children who are buying a four/

> **'There could easily be 50 people involved, each with a crucial role at some point.'**

Be tenacious in your attempts to keep everything moving forwards. You can't be organised enough nor afraid to pester everyone involved in the chain - see pages 161-2 for advice on how to keep on top of everything.

five-bedroom property to which they will add a granny flat for his mother. They are buying from …

■ **E:** … a couple who are separating and selling their home to finance two smaller properties, one owned by …

■ **F:** … an older couple downsizing to a smaller bungalow on the coast currently owned by …

■ **G:** … an elderly woman who is moving into a nursing home. The other property the Es are buying is a three-bedroom semi-detached owned by …

■ **H:** … a couple retiring to a Spanish villa being built by a developer.

Spend a moment thinking about each person in the chain and you can conjure up many reasons why they might change their mind, try to delay progress, or just run out of money. The chain will only progress at the pace of the slowest link. The tricky bit is knowing who that is at any one stage and encouraging them to get a move on.

How to avoid getting in a chain

With the right preparation and research, there are times when you can avoid being in a chain, or at least a long one.

■ **Buy from a developer** offering part exchange, so they buy your property and there is no one further up the chain.

■ **Sell your property** and go into short-term rented accommodation, or if you are

lucky, house-sit a friend's home or stay with friends or relatives. Then, as a cash buyer, choose vendors whose chain is short, or who are themselves prepared to move out and rent. You'll need to put a lot of your belongings into storage.

■ **Buy an already** empty property.

■ **If you can,** choose a buyer who isn't in a chain themselves.

■ **Only make offers** where the chain is short.

■ **Negotiate a move-in date** with your vendor, after which they are prepared to move out, whatever their circumstances, or the deal will be off.

> **'The chain will only progress at the pace of the slowest link.'**

How to keep a chain moving

Buyers and sellers who are part of a chain often feel that it is the job of the professionals to keep communicating and ensuring the right things are happening: they feel excluded from the process. However, there is no formal structure to a chain and so it often comes down to pot luck and one individual taking it upon him or herself to check, remind and nag others to turn their paperwork around. Some agents do a good job here, and wise agents – big and small – have dedicated sales progression departments.

Why do chains fail?

■ **Poor communication:** someone doesn't get around to signing or filling in a document, and no one chases them up.

■ **A buyer or a seller** changes their mind about the deal and pulls out.

■ **A buyer** can't get a loan to match the offer they made.

■ **A legal firm** with too many cases on its books only reviews each case once a week, sends out the relevant letters, then only chases them up a week later after the next review.

■ **A survey** reveals problems, which prompt the buyer to pull out or the mortgage company to hold back part of the loan.

■ **The survey** requires further specialist surveys, such as timber and damp, or the services of a structural engineer.

> '**Some vendors seem to have no compunction about taking their house off the market at a surprisingly late stage.**'

■ **Couples split up** and pull out of a sale or purchase.

■ **A buyer or seller** falls ill or loses their job, pulling out of a deal as a result.

Gazumping

Gazumping is when your vendor accepts your offer but then agrees a higher price with another buyer. It is not as common as media stories suggest, but it can happen. Prevent it by making your offer subject to the property being taken off the market for an agreed period while you both sort out the paperwork to exchange. As a vendor, make sure you only do this for someone who can prove they have a Mortgage Agreement in Principle and are in a position to purchase the property – such as a cash buyer.

Some vendors seem to have no compunction about taking their house off the market at surprisingly late stages. There is little you can do about this, but since their agent will not be paid unless the sale goes through, in an ideal world they wouldn't market a property they did not believe the vendor wants to sell. Sadly this doesn't happen and the agent often gets caught out. Estate agents are legally obliged to pass on all offers, so someone who viewed the property before you put in an offer can still make a bid.

The opposite of gazumping is gazundering. For more information, see page 207. If you feel you have been unfairly treated by an estate agent, go to pages 180–1 where there is information on dealing with disputes.

How to manage the chain

Look through the checklist that appears opposite for why a chain can fail and make sure none of it applies to you. You should also help the rest of the chain by making sure that you follow as much of the following information as possible.

Here are some ways to help to keep on top of everything:

- **Employ a good,** experienced agent and a legal specialist.
- **Get your finances in place early,** especially cash for your deposit at time of exchange.
- **File everything,** including copies of your correspondence and notes of telephone conversations. Keep copies of contact details of services at work, just in case.
- **Have copies of documents** that are likely to be requested, planning permission, building regulation certificates, plans of drainage etc.
- **Turn around** your paperwork as promptly as possible.
- **Deliver documents** by hand, courier or special delivery.
- **Put clauses** in your buying and selling contracts stating the dates by which you should exchange, have the survey done, and complete.
- **If you are part of a couple,** share out the jobs to avoid any confusion or duplicated work and calls to other people in the chain.

> 'Employ experienced professionals, keep on top of the paperwork and get your finances in place early on.'

We become more stressed if not enough time is put aside to provide all the paperwork for sale, or read it for buying. In addition, to make sure you know and understand what's happening, put several days aside to spend reviewing and asking questions. Talk to your representatives regularly – at least once a week – and ask if there is

BE CAREFUL!

If your survey reveals a problem that was not apparent in the your mortgage valuation, don't panic. All types of faults can seem horrendous in writing, but they can be fixed. Get a builder or specialist's opinion and discuss it with your vendor: they will want to be flexible to keep the sale going, so you should be able to renegotiate the price to allow for the work required.

anything they or you should be doing next and by when. Ask where there are problems and who should be dealing with them. If someone needs to be hurried along, ask if you are allowed to give them a ring, or who will and when they will get back to you. Keep a list of everyone's contact details (landlines, mobiles, faxes, email and postal addresses) so that you can get in touch if you need to. Be tenacious and proactive and try to treat the process as you would a business deal.

All this is going to take time, and be emotionally draining. If possible, reduce your other workload and commitments so that you are available – for example, put off foreign trips! Be flexible: if your buyer finds flaws with the property, consider the problem. You might be able to deal with it yourself or you might decide it merits negotiation on price. Remember that the agent will probably have come across such problems before and should have some advice for you.

> 'Get involved with the process to help avoid becoming stressed. Be tenacious and proactive and try to treat the process as you would a business deal.'

Getting to the exchange stage

Exchange of contracts is when the copies of the signed contracts are swapped between the two legal firms and a deposit is made by the buyer to the vendor. It is the point at which an agreement to buy or sell becomes legally binding. Once everyone in the chain has exchanged, you're on the home straight because no one can back out of their deal. At this point a date should be set for completion and a legal firm can be sued if they fail to meet that date, so they have a strong incentive to meet the deadline. However, most delays occur on the route to exchange.

All of the following stages need to be completed for you to exchange contracts:

- **Property title deeds** drawn down from the lender of the property for sale.
- **Preliminary enquiries** and local searches.
- **Fixtures and fittings form** and property information forms filled in and signed.
- **Key information from any leasehold documents,** such as special clauses prohibiting pets and subletting.
- **Survey** and any resulting actions or negotiations.
- **Other negotiations** (e.g. on fixtures and fittings).
- **Answers** to all 'buyers questions'.
- **Written mortgage offer.**
- **Contracts** for sale and purchase drawn up.

- **Agreed deposit** available.
- **Completion** date agreed.
- **Buildings insurance** in place by the buyer.

When buying, you become legally responsible for the property's building insurance once you exchange, so you will need to have this arranged and pass the policy number and a copy of the policy to your legal firm. It is worth asking the vendor who their policy is with as you may want to continue with that insurer. This is a particularly good idea if the property is in a flood risk area or has subsidence problems as the insurer will already have details on the building and associated risks.

Setting a completion date

There are many other jobs to do between finalising the legal agreement and moving in, so it makes sense to agree a completion date at least two weeks after exchange; for a smooth move, try for four weeks. Unless someone is going into rented or borrowed accommodation, everyone in the chain moves house on completion day, or a day or two after. Try not to complete on a Friday, because conveyancing and removals firms tend to be booked up on that day, and, also, if there are delays with

finances, you could be stranded for a whole weekend and end up paying for your goods to be stored over that time. You also need to decide how you will move and choose a removals firm (see pages 168–9).

You may want to arrange to visit your new property so you can take measurements to see if your curtains and loose carpets will fit, and to check if there is room for your kitchen appliances, such as the fridge. You should also notify your 'contents' insurance provider of when and where you will be moving and check with them what is/is not insured during the move, as you may need to get additional insurance from them, or via the removal company (see also page 169).

Reaching completion

Completion is when the remaining money is paid by the buyer and the mortgage company and you get the keys to your new property over which you took ownership when you exchanged. That's why you can't complete without having exchanged contracts, although on very rare occasions completion and exchange can happen at the same time. Your role in completion is to wait nervously for the phone call telling you all is well. The list overleaf explains where the money is paid from.

See pages 64–6 for advice on choosing buildings insurance. You won't be able to exchange contracts on a property until this is organised so you obviously need to get it up front.

- **Any balance** left after your mortgage is paid off with the funds from your purchaser.
- **Your new loan.**
- **Your own cash.**

The money is transferred electronically between the legal firms' bank accounts, each one triggering the next transfer. This all takes time and if you are near the top of the chain, the system may run out of time in transferring funds, so have a contingency plan for where you could stay overnight if you have handed over the keys but have nowhere to go. This is another reason to try to avoid completing on Fridays, as unfinished business will then be left to the following Monday.

If the money hits the bank by 12pm and the vendors have moved, you can move in. So once money is in the bank, you should be able to move in (or have moved out) by 2pm.

> **'Have a contingency plan for where you could stay overnight if you have handed over the keys but have nowhere to go.'**

Buy some time if you can

The few days after you move into your new property are an ideal time to change any superficial decoration you don't like, put up new cupboards, curtains and some familiar pictures, and clean out anything that isn't up to your standards. If you are able to arrange a couple of days between completion and moving in (maybe with your belongings going into storage), you can get a lot more done in an empty property.

When selling, however, never hand over the keys until your legal firm tells you they have completed. Waiting for that call can be nerve wracking. If it doesn't come, call your legal firm and find out why. There could be a hitch, such as someone suddenly falling ill, in which case you may all have to wait another day. If this is the case, you may need to negotiate who is covering the costs of this, such as hotel and storage charges.

If you are releasing cash from your sale, make sure you let the solicitor know where to send the money and have a plan of what you are going to do with it.

Preparing for move day

7

Preparation is the key to a smooth moving day that is as stress free as possible. This chapter explains how getting professional help can save your sanity and your back. As always, who you choose is crucial and there is guidance on this, as well as how to stay organised in the run-up to the big day.

Getting organised

Moving day can be the day when all the stress of selling and buying a property is multiplied tenfold. You can do a lot to lower the anxiety levels, but they won't disappear altogether: it will be physically tiring and emotionally draining.

The first step can be taken weeks ahead of your move: clear out everything you don't use or need. You'll otherwise be paying money to move stuff that you don't want and which is going to clutter up your new home. With a bit of luck, you could raise enough at a car boot sale to pay your removals costs. Think about where your furniture will be going in the new property, and check that it will fit. If it won't fit, sell it, give it away or take it to the dump now. Check what you've got stacked in the loft and other storage spaces, such as the garage or shed, and dispense with what you don't need.

> 'Think about where your furniture will be going in the new property, and check that it will fit.'

You'll have to decide early on if you are going to use a removals firm, and if you are going to get them to do the packing. The decision is needed now because if you pack yourself, it could take weeks.

Do you want a removals firm?

If you live in a ground floor one-bedroom flat with little clutter, you can hire a van, get a couple of friends to help, and move yourself on the day. If you've got more than four rooms to empty, there's probably too much to do. Consider how many possessions you have. What's hidden away in the loft or the garden shed? It can come as a big shock to discover how many goods you have accumulated. Now imagine having to pick up each one of them, carry it across an obstacle course (including stairs) and put it down without breaking your back – and all to a deadline.

 Take a look at the countdown checklist on page 172 for prompts for what you need to be thinking about several weeks before the move itself. You can't start planning for the day soon enough.

Moving yourself

If you decide you can move yourself, book the largest van you can (anything over 7.5 tonnes when loaded requires an HGV licence). Ask for one with a low kerb height or a let-down tailboard for ease of loading. Remember you'll probably have to make several journeys, including a final one to return the van, so this is only practical for moves over a fairly short distance. Loading and unloading to a 12 noon deadline will be tiring and you might not relish the subsequent unpacking and setting up required over the next few weeks in your new property.

Leader of the pack

A major disadvantage of packing yourself is the time it takes, leaving you in a sweaty panic on moving day, or doing without key possessions for weeks ahead of the move.

So, well in advance of the move, buy or hire packing cases – they are stronger than cardboard boxes and it's easier to pack containers of the same size. Start by packing the things you won't need before the move. Depending on the time of year, this could be gardening equipment, summer clothes, etc.

Wear gloves when packing – it's amazing how much dirt collects on

> **'It is worth labelling all boxes with a brief description of their contents and the intended room.'**

your hands otherwise. Put layers of crumpled paper or other protective material between each item to prevent scratching. Check the box is not too heavy and label it clearly with its contents and which floor and room it should go to. Draw an arrow to show which way up it should be stored.

Don't overfill boxes with heavy items: put heavy things on the bottom and lighter items on the top. Keep hazardous substances such as household cleaners and decorating supplies in separate boxes to other goods and mark 'hazardous'.

When carrying heavy items, take extreme care and try not to put any strain on your back – keep it straight as much as possible. Watch out for jolts from uneven surfaces and things left on the floor.

Nuts and bolts advice

When dismantling furniture, put all the screws, nuts and bolts in a labelled clear plastic bag and tape it to one of the pieces.

Packing box suppliers include: **www.helpineedboxes.co.uk**, **www.removal-supply.co.uk** and **www.ekmpowershop.co.uk**. Or you can go into any storage company, such as Access or Big Yellow, and buy them from there.

Choosing a removals firm

Amazingly, only about a quarter of people who are moving opt for a professional removal company that is a member of the British Association of Removers. Using a 'man with a van' or cheaper services can be a false economy.

While the pressure to save money is understandable at this time, the cost in creaking backs and strained relationships is immeasurable.

Calling on the professionals to move your possessions may seem a little extreme at a time when you are probably trying to save money – surely it's not that difficult a job? It's true, moving items may not be that difficult, but there is an art to:

- Packing items correctly so that breakable items are properly protected.
- Knowing how much weight each box (and you) can carry.
- Making sure the van is packed so that boxes and items do not move in transit and break.
- Being realistic about how long the job will take. Cheaper services tend to add to your pressure by not giving enough time for the job.

And remember, you already have a lot to do on moving day and you may need to be out of your home and on your way by 12 noon–2pm! Using a professional firm means:

- **Your possessions** are packed properly and insured in transit.
- **Trained staff** can pack fast, probably only a day or two ahead of the move.
- **You don't have to lift** and carry heavy or bulky items, so you are free to deal with the many other jobs that need doing before and on the day of the move.

There are plenty of horror stories about sloppy removals men, but most firms do a professional job. Go for a member of the British

Access problems

Heavy or tall lorries can't always cope with steep gradients, tight bends or uneven roads. Check if there are access or parking problems at the other end – you may need to contact the police to get permission to unload, or to have a parking meter suspended.

 Removals firm websites include: **www.bar.co.uk**; **www.removalsombudsman. org.uk** (check the firm you choose is a member); **www.ngrs.co.uk** and **www.fidi.com**.

Association of Removers or one that is covered by the Removals Ombudsman (see box, below).

Always get more than one estimate of the cost, preferably from someone coming to the property rather than going online. This is because there may be problems with access, or very tight stairways, which will affect the job. If you are moving to a new area, it may be worth getting an estimate from a firm based where you are going: prices there may be more competitive. Make sure you mention all the items you want moved, including the contents of a loft or garage.

Ask for the estimate to be broken down so that you can see what you are paying for. You can usefully ask to see insurance, packing, hourly rate, mileage and any storage costs. This will help you compare costs between estimates accurately. Find out if overtime rates apply and at what time they start. Ask what would happen if the move is delayed and you couldn't get into the new property in the afternoon or the next day.

Check, too, that they have adequate insurance cover and also what the time limit is on claiming on insurance after the move. If you have some high value possessions, check if they need special packing and if they will also be covered by insurance (some policies set a limit per item).

You can still choose to do some of the packing yourself, which will save on costs, but steer clear of packing breakables and remember the removal firms insurance will not cover items you pack. Ask the firm to supply packing cases a few weeks in advance, and if they can't, go to the websites listed on page 167. If the distance of your move is short, you may be able to transport some items yourself, saving on costs.

Briefing a removals firm

Once you have chosen the firm, prepare and send them a briefing sheet to include:

- **Any items** needing special packing, such as pictures, antiques and valuable objects.
- **Difficult to move items,** such as a piano or fish tank.
- **Wardrobes** or other large furniture that may need to be dismantled.
- **Any carpets** and curtains that are going.
- **Items** you will be taking yourself.
- **A layout** of the new property with rooms identified, so that they/you can label boxes with their destination. Colour coding can work well as it is quick to do and easy to understand.

 To obtain a removal quote online, visit **http://residential.bishopsmove.com** and **www.rightmove.co.uk/removals.html.**

I'm moving

There is a vast list of organisations that you need to inform. It therefore makes sense to send them a standard letter with a gap for you to add relevant reference and account details. See the table on page 172 for suggested timings.

As well as all the organisations and people listed opposite, tell the post office so that mail will be redirected. You'll need a form available from www.postoffice.co.uk, by phone or from a post office branch. It takes up to ten days to come into effect. Prepare change of address cards for friends and family.

If you are changing your phone number, you can also arrange for your telephone company to automatically inform callers of your new number for a few weeks following the switch-over date.

Freeze yourself out
Run down the contents of your freezer, and only buy fresh food for a few weeks before the move to help you to use up frozen and stored foods.

Transferring services
Ten days ahead of your projected move, make sure all utility services, such as water, gas and electricity, are informed that you will be moving. Ask them to arrange to read the meters on the move day. Ring to check this will happen. If they can't do it themselves, ask a qualified electrician to do a reading so you have an independent record, or take a date-stamped digital photograph of your meter reading. Moving house is a good time to review your arrangements with utilities. You can compare tariffs at www.which. co.uk/switch and www.uswitch. co.uk. You can also transfer your landline phone number to your new address for a charge.

Most companies will have a special telephone number to call to advise that you are moving or you can contact them in writing and, more frequently, by the internet.

Redirection services are offered by **www.royalmail.com** and **www.iammoving. com**. They do this free of charge but may pass on your information for direct marketing purposes unless you specify that they can't. On the plus side, you may save some time, expense and hassle.

Organisations and people to contact with change of address details

As soon as you have an approximate idea of when you will be moving, contact the following organisations either by email or letter so that everything is set out in writing. This list is by no means exhaustive; there are bound to be additions relating to your circumstances. Some organisations, such as banks, may require you to fill in their own forms.

Government organisations

- Department for Work and Pensions
- Inland Revenue
- VAT office

Finance

- Your bank and credit card firms
- Savings and investment firms, such as National Savings and Investment Premium Bonds
- Pension services
- Store loyalty cards

Insurance

- Contents and building (and see car)

Suppliers

- Water, gas, electricity
- Landline phone and broadband company
- Sky/cable/TV licence
- Magazine subscriptions

Car

- DVLA, for both your licence and the vehicle registration, but don't do this before you move as you may need your licence for identification and van hire
- Car insurance, MOT
- Breakdown service

Health

- Doctor, dentist, optician, plus any other specialists

Work, education and leisure

- Your employer and professional associations
- Your colleagues
- Schools and colleges
- Clubs
- Football pools
- Local newsletters
- Other mailing lists (theatres, catalogues, charities)

Countdown checklists

Four weeks ahead

- Get removals estimates and book your chosen firm (even with a provisional date)
- Order packing cases
- Order new curtains/carpets for the property
- Plan where furniture will go and dispose of unwanted items
- Book the days needed off work

Two weeks ahead

- Inform utility companies
- Complete the mail redirection form
- Inform TV signal supplier and TV licence
- Start packing non-essentials – start outside or at the top of the house
- Run down the freezer

One week ahead

- Inform the people on the finance and medical lists
- Tell your council and ask for a statement on your Council Tax – you may get a refund
- Inform the car and household insurance firms
- Send out change of address cards to friends and family
- Organise who will look after pets or children during the move
- Transfer into pots any plants you've said you will be taking

Two days ahead

- Defrost the freezer
- Prepare your 'essentials' box (see page 174)
- Set aside things you will be transporting
- Disconnect dishwasher (if removals men are not doing it)
- Label items and keys for the new owner
- Take down any curtains and light fittings you are taking with you

After moving

- Pay Stamp Duty Land Tax (see page 177)
- Change locks

Make sure you have a receipt or record of them being notified by you as the utility companies can make mistakes and if they do, you are still liable for the bill unless you can prove you notified them and they have received it.

Information for the new owner

It is very helpful if you prepare a briefing sheet for the new owner. This should include how to operate the boiler and alarm, the location of the meters, fuse box and stopcock, and any other useful information. You could either label all keys or leave them in the lock that they operate. Don't forget the shed and garage keys, or those that operate the window locks.

And don't forget to ask – or have it as part of your purchase agreement – that the person you are buying from does the same.

On the day

If you can take it, have a big breakfast as mealtimes are likely to be disrupted today. Put down sheets to protect the floor as people traipse in and out. The removals men are likely to turn up early and they work very fast, so if you are dismantling furniture or disconnecting appliances, do it the day before they arrive. Check the foreman knows the brief (give him a copy if necessary). Get his mobile phone number in case of emergencies (remember, you'll be travelling separately).

'Prepare a briefing sheet for the new owner with key information for keys and alarms.'

Strip the beds. Get the electricity and gas meters read (if it has to be you, get someone to witness you reading and sign the paper, or take a photograph of the meter – it might help if there is a dispute). Set aside the vacuum cleaner and cleaning equipment for your last-minute clear up or, better still, ask a friend or cleaner to do the work for you.

If you have young children, take them to whoever is caring for them until you move. Do the same with any pets. If you know where you are in the chain, you will have some idea of when you are likely to hear you have completed, as it will work up from the bottom. So if you are a first-time buyer at the start of the chain, you should be able to move as early as 12 noon. And if you are selling to first-time buyers,

Home sweet home

It will help your whole family to settle in if the new place feels like home. One way to help with this is to set aside a small stock of pictures (so take some picture hooks and a hammer), other familiar objects and, if possible, curtains. Take these in your car as you are likely to arrive before the removals lorry. When you get into the new property, put them in place as soon as you can: the surroundings will feel more like your home, which can lift everyone's spirits at a time when you are most likely feeling tired and drained.

Essentials box

Keep aside a clearly labelled box of things you need to help you survive the day. This could include:

- Kettle (with flex), teabags, coffee, milk and sugar
- Soft drinks
- Snacks, such as biscuits or fruit
- Sandwiches or flask of soup for lunch
- Toiletries, headache pills and any other medication
- Toilet paper
- Spare light bulbs in case they are needed in the new property
- Gloves if you are going to be loading or unloading
- Paper and pens to label rooms in the new property
- Map of where you are going
- Your property contacts list.

be prepared to be out by then! The poor people further along the line will have to wait.

As soon as the house is empty, zoom around it for a last-minute clean up. Do not leave the house until your legal firm advises you to, and drop off the keys with the agent.

Your new home

When you get in, label or colour code each room so the removals men know what will go where. Be clear about where you want any heavy furniture put. Don't expect to unpack anything but the bare essentials: bedding and a meal (and you might prefer a takeaway). Don't forget everyone will be tired when moving your items in, so make sure you know what goes

where and be around to direct the moving in process. You may realise you need to clean items such as kitchen cupboards or shelves before stacking anything in them.

Take readings of any gas and electricity meters as a record in case of any dispute with the supplier. As with leaving your sold property, if possible, photograph the figures, or write them down and get someone to witness your writing.

Your removals team will expect a tip, and you will most likely feel they've earned it. If there is a problem with their work, tell the foreman. You may be asked to sign to confirm the job is completed (check the van!) and if you haven't yet inspected your belongings, note that they are unexamined. This will help if there is a dispute later.

Be prepared to feel tired and maybe a bit let down: you probably haven't seen the property empty or noticed blemishes on walls that were hidden behind furniture. Try to stay positive and remember what it is that attracted you to the property in the first place.

Cool customer

Fridges are supposed to be left switched off on a level surface for 24 hours after being moved to allow their gas systems to settle. Whether you choose to do this is up to you, but try to get the fridge installed early on to give it as much time as possible before being operated.

Settling in

8

It's not over yet! This chapter deals with the 'must do' jobs after moving in, and offers guidance on what you need to do from now on to make sure your next move is easier. This is also your chance to review how the move went and deal with any complaints or disputes with the other people and firms involved.

File your paperwork

Phew! Once you've had time to get used to your new home, think back over the whole selling and buying process and consider what went well and what didn't.

Consider what you could have done to make it easier. Did the people working on your behalf do a good job? If they did, make a note that you'd use them again and recommend them to friends. If they didn't, you may want to make a complaint.

The first thing to do is to file all the paperwork to do with the process. This will help you in making judgements about how to do it better next time, and also, very importantly, help you retain the information for the next time you sell your property. Your file will hold essential information when you come to sell, even if you don't move for ten years. So make sure you include in it:

- The sale particulars of your home
- The EPC
- Your buildings and contents insurance
- Any estimates from builders and other tradesmen for work to be done
- Safety certificates, warranties and guarantees.

As well as all correspondence and notes about your:

- Agent
- Survey
- Legal firm
- Mortgage

You should also keep an ongoing record of any decoration you undertake. This should include the source and code numbers of paints, flooring and carpets. You'll

> **'The first thing to do is to file all the paperwork to do with the process. This will help you in making judgements about how to do it better next time.'**

The Stamp Duty Land Tax help line is 0845 603 0135 or website **www.hmrc. gov.uk**. To contact the Land Registry go to **www.landregistry.gov.uk**. There are regional phone numbers listed on this site.

Pay Stamp Duty Land Tax

- Stamp Duty Land Tax (SDLT) replaced stamp duty in December 2003, and is now the responsibility of the property owner who can, if they wish, ask their legal firm to deal with it (some will charge about £50 for this service). If you agree a fixed fee for your conveyancing, as a lot of people do now, this may well be included as part of that service.

- It entails filling in a land transaction return form called SDLT1, available online or by post from the Inland Revenue (see box at foot of the page, opposite).

- You or your legal firm can complete the form, and you have to sign it because you (not your representative) are held responsible if any of the information in it is wrong.

- Send it to the Inland Revenue together with your payment. No payment is required on properties sold for up to £125,000. After that, the rates are as outlined below.

- The Inland Revenue then issue you (or your legal firm, if you choose) with a certificate. This must be passed on to the Land Registry (also see box opposite) so that you can be registered as the owner of the property.

- The completed form and payment must be submitted within 30 days of the date of completion (date of settlement in Scotland), or you are liable for a £100 fine. For the latest SDLT rates, visit the website: www.hmrc.gov.uk/sdlt/rates-tables.htm.

Stamp Duty Land Tax charges

The current (April 2012) stamp duty rates are:

Selling price	SDLT charge
Up to £125,000	Nil
Over £125,000 to £250,000	1 per cent
Over £250,000 to £500,000	3 per cent
Over £500,000 to £1 million	4 per cent
Over £1 million to £2 million	5 per cent
Over £2 million	7 per cent

be grateful for this when you want to touch up the paintwork in three years time and can't remember which shade it was!

Before you leave a property, make sure you collect keys from all your friends and neighbours. Also consider changing the locks on a new property for peace of mind.

Create a new home moving file

Make sure you keep all essential paperwork such as guarantees, certificates and utility services in the same place. Contact details for any useful tradesmen that have worked on the property in the past are helpful too.

Maintenance

Do bear in mind that all property requires maintenance. The survey or home condition report should identify any future work.

The surveyor should be able to advise you what needs doing and perhaps recommend a tradesman. Alternatively, go to the relevant tradesman organisation, such

Jargon buster

Federation of Master Builders Builders trade association.
NICEIC A voluntary organisation set up to monitor standards and safety of electrical contractors.
Stamp Duty Land Tax (SDLT) Tax paid when you buy a property.

as the **Federation of Master Builders** (FMB) (www.fmb.org.uk), Trustmark, Which? Local (http://local.which.co.uk/) or the **NICEIC** (www.niceic.org.uk). Whatever work you arrange, note it and keep the guarantees, warranties or safety certificates. If you can't produce them for say electrical work, you could have to get it done again.

BE CAREFUL!
If you've become a property owner for the first time, it is sensible to make a will or amend your existing one to help deal with your estate if you die.

For further help on tradesman institutions and organisations go to **www.trustmark.org.uk** and **www.designsonproperty.co.uk**. Which? Local is a free website for Which? subscribers to recommend local service providers they have used and rate them. To find out more, visit **http://local.which.co.uk**.

Dealing with disputes

Mistakes can happen and problems can arise when dealing with anyone. There are generally ways around mishaps, but if the matter becomes more serious you need to know what procedures to follow. Read on for such information.

A lot of things can go wrong in the process of buying and selling property. Much of the time these problems are caused by lack of communication or preparation. The process also tends to bring out the worst in people: sellers and buyers can be greedy and may try to change the terms to get a better deal. Sometimes the professionals get caught up in this, and, of course, sometimes they make mistakes or don't behave to the highest standards. If you want to make a complaint about any of the services you received, follow these rules:

- **Be clear** about what went wrong and what you want done about it – do you want an apology, a reduced charge, or compensation?
- **Follow the company's** complaints procedure. This is most likely to begin with you explaining the complaint in writing to the people who did the work. If they do not deal with it to your satisfaction, go further up their organisation. If you're still not happy, go to their regulatory body or to an Ombudsman, if they are a member of one.
- **Keep copies** of all correspondence and notes of phone calls, including who you spoke to and when.
- **Be firm** but polite.
- **Set reasonable deadlines** for a response to your complaint.

> **'Sellers and buyers can be greedy and may try to get a better deal. The professionals can get caught up in this or make their own mistakes.'**

Organisations that help and advise on complaints include **www.tradingstandards.gov.uk, www.citizensadvice.org.uk** and **www.howtocomplain.com.**

All of the firms you deal with will be aware that you could be a future customer, and that many people ask their friends for recommendations, so it will be in their interest to deal with your complaint.

Disputes with your estate agent

The most common complaint against estate agents is about their charges. You may feel these do not match the level of service you received, or you may get a nasty surprise when you see the bill. Check the wording of the contract you signed against the terms explained on pages 100–1. If there are extra charges on top of the fee, look to see if the contract alerted you to them.

If the charges reflect what is stated in the contract it is unlikely you have grounds to complain, but there is never any harm in laying out what you feel the company has done wrong and that you would like to have it put right. If they belong to a governing body (see box opposite below), then they may be able to advise you.

'The most common complaint against estate agents is about their charges. Check the wording of the contract you signed and if there are extra charges, check if the contract alerted you to them.'

You may have other complaints. Did the agent check your buyer's financial credibility? Was their market valuation accurate – if the property sold very fast you were either lucky or underpriced. If it took a long time or you had to drop the asking price, maybe they – and you – were too ambitious. However, if you went against their advice in opting for a very high asking price, you can hardly complain now. Were the sales particulars accurate? Did they pass on offers in writing or just on the phone (all offers should be communicated in writing)? Were they efficient in handling viewers' appointments and queries? These are all complaints about the service you paid for. If you feel it was poor, note this and don't use them again or recommend them.

The website www.which.co.uk/agentproblems provides advice for dealing with a variety of complaints made against estate agents.

Disputes with your surveyor

As a buyer, you may well have paid for a survey on the property you purchased. If you discover a serious problem with the structure, damp or dry rot, read the survey and check if it was identified. If it wasn't, contact the surveyor and ask them to visit the property.

If they agree there is a fault that isn't in their report, or that they didn't indicate needed further investigation or was exempt from their survey, they should offer to

Disputes with your legal firm

If you are surprised by extra charges in your legal bill, check your original estimate. Sometimes these do not include search fees or electronic bank transfers. Other grounds for complaint are usually the speed of work and the quality of communication. These should not be issues if you followed the advice on selecting a legal firm on page 109 and managing the chain on pages 159–63, but if they are, follow the firm's complaints procedure. It is worth asking the legal firm at the outset how long the conveyancing is likely to take, and for warnings of any delays.

To make a complaint about legal work, you must start by writing to the person who was responsible for it. If that doesn't work, go to the firm's complaints officer. The third stage is the complaints service of the Law Society where the firm is based: England and Wales, Scotland or Northern Ireland. If you are still unhappy you can go to an ombudsman: The Legal Services Ombudsman in England and Wales, or the Scottish Legal Services Ombudsman, or the Lay Observer in Northern Ireland (see box, below).

> '**If you discover a serious problem with the structure, damp or dry rot, read the survey to check if it was identified.**'

compensate you, ideally by fixing the problem.

They may argue that they did not have access to the area where the fault was apparent (the survey report is likely to have a clause explaining that the inspection cannot include difficult to access areas, such as under nailed down carpets or attics with no ladder). If so, ask if they have a 'hidden defects' policy. This policy covers the surveyor in such a situation.

All members of the Royal Institution of Chartered Surveyors (RICS) are part of its arbitration scheme. A trained arbitrator studies submissions by both parties and examines the evidence, sometimes including a visit to the property. If you choose to use it, you will have to pay over £300.

 Ideally sort out your complaint with the agent and their trade organisation (for example, the National Association of Estate Agents, **www.naea.co.uk**) first. If this does not work, go to one of the approved redress schemes, such as the Property Ombudsman (**www.tpos.co.uk**).

If you have lost money due to poor conveyancing (perhaps by not being able to move into a property, or suffered an unreasonable delay caused by your solicitor), you may have a claim for negligence. This will initially be dealt with by the relevant law society (see box, opposite below), but you will eventually require the services of a solicitor in order to sue your provider.

Disputes with your seller

If you find some fixtures or fittings that were supposed to stay have been removed, or vice versa, inform your solicitor and check they will deal with this as part of the service. They may be able to help, but, sadly you have little practical comeback once the property has changed hands, and it is only worth the trouble if you feel very strongly about it.

Case study Mr and Mrs Bassett

Most of the complaints you hear about are to do with estate agents or, indeed, surveyors who may have missed something when checking a property. However, one of the professions whose errors are not always well publicised is the legal profession. Most do a good job, but in this instance, one of the solicitors tried to blame everyone else for not exchanging – but got caught!

In this case, a first-time buyer was buying a property, and the vendor of this property buying another. The second property being sold was the last one in the 'chain' as the couple (Mr and Mrs Bassett) were moving into rented accommodation. So there were just two agents, three solicitors and a surveyor involved.

This short chain should have exchanged within weeks, but just at the last minute there was a problem in that one of the solicitors had apparently forgotten to request more documents from a vendor.

Becoming suspicious over what was happening, Mr and Mrs Bassett decided to find out what was holding up the exchange. They rang their solicitor to find out where the problem was. He spoke to the buyer's solicitor and was told they were ready to exchange, but were being held up by the first-time buyer's solicitor. Angry at this, the Bassetts rang the agent who was selling the first property and asked if they could speak to the first-time buyer's solicitor to speed them up. A slightly confused estate agent rang back quickly to say that she had been told the reason for the delay was not the first-time buyer's solicitor, but that the middle solicitor was blaming them for the hold-up!

It soon became apparent that the solicitor who was the only one handling a sale and purchase was blaming the others for not being ready. The exchange was then concluded a few hours later after an ultimatum was sent. As there was no financial loss incurred, no further action was taken.

Disputes with your removals firm

There are some terrible horror stories about items being lost or damaged during a move or while they were in storage. Such incidents can be very upsetting as possessions can also have emotional value. If you used a reputable firm that is a member of a trade association or the removals ombudsman scheme (see box, below), the chances are all went well, and if it didn't, at least you've got someone to complain to who can help.

If the company doesn't create an inventory as part of the service, it's sensible to create one yourself. Try to get a representative of the company to sign the inventory as this will help if there is a dispute at any point over what was on board the removal lorry.

Keep a written note of anything being broken or damaged during the move and ask the foreman to sign it. Of course, you might not notice such events at the time, but aim to unpack as soon as you can and list anything that is broken or damaged as you find it. Take photographs of damaged goods as further evidence, particularly if you believe they were poorly packed. Immediately contact the firm and

'If the removals firm doesn't create an inventory as part of the service, it's sensible to create one yourself. Try to get a representative of the company to sign it as this will help if there is a dispute at any point.'

the insurers to inform them that you will be making a claim. Keep receipts for repairs or replacements to support your claim.

You might be offered a small sum in compensation on the grounds that the goods were used. Some firms also have a limit on how much you can claim per item – check this at the time of booking (see page 169) and also the basis on which they will replace/ pay for damaged items – will it be new for old or like for like?

If you don't feel you are being offered enough, say so. It may be that you are covered by your insurance firm, too, so check with them what the situation is and if they will pay out or help you to recover monies owed from the removal company.

Relevant legal websites are: **www.clc-uk.org**; **www.lawsociety.org.uk** (for England and Wales); **www.lawscot.org.uk** (for Scotland); **www.lawsoc-ni.org** (for Northern Ireland); **www.lawsociety.ie** (for Ireland); **www.olso.org** (Legal Services Ombudsman); **www.slso.org.uk** (Scottish Legal Services Ombudsman) and **www.adrnow.org.uk** (Northern Ireland Lay Observer).

Making claims

If you discover that work such as timber treatment or damp proofing is faulty, check your paperwork for any guarantees.

If the firm has since gone out of business (sadly very common), it's not worth the paper it is written on. However, the Guarantee Protection Insurance Company provides insurance cover in specialist areas of building, and insures work done by members of the Property Care Association (formerly the British Wood and Damp-proofing Association) so check if the firm were or are members. There is information about the ten-year warranty offered on new properties on page 130. It is also worth checking that any guarantee is transferable to future purchasers of the property and isn't just for the benefit of the owner that had the work done.

However, it's only been since 31 March 2003 that free guarantees have been legally enforceable. So even if the company is still trading and the guarantee is transferable, if the company refuses to honour a free guarantee (issued before this date), then there may be little in practice you can do about it. The exception is Scotland, where even prior to this date a promise was legally enforceable.

> **'If you discover that work such as timber treatment or damp proofing is faulty, check your paperwork for any guarantees.'**

Websites for organisations who regulate removals firms are: **www.bar.co.uk** (British Association of Removers) and **www.removalsombudsman.org.uk**. For the Guarantee Protection Insurance Ltd go to **www.gptprotection.co.uk** and for the Property Care Association, go to **www.property-care.org**.

Selling and buying in Scotland

9

The property buying and selling process is different in Scotland and this chapter takes you through each stage explaining the differences. With a system based around binding bids, it is imperative that you thoroughly research the property you are interested in before handing over the envelope that could seal your fate.

Selling in Scotland

The residential property market in Scotland is worth about £23 billion annually. According to Registers for Scotland, the average selling price remains similar year on year, being £153,500 in the second quarter of 2011 to £153,825 in 2012.

Scottish buyers enjoyed a better run on property prices than England and didn't start to get hit by declines until 2008. Since then, however, prices have fallen by around 18 per cent on average across Scotland, which is similar to the rest of the UK. Scottish buyers used to the system of finding a property first, putting an offer in with an agreed date to buy and then selling up, now have to plan much further ahead.

First check that sufficient funds can be secured to purchase a property with a mortgage. Once this has been done, think about selling your property first and agree a date to move that will tie in with the purchase of your next home. If you agree to purchase a property before selling your own, you need to make sure that you don't have to move for at least another six months, rather than the previous system of selling and moving in 12–16 weeks. Above

all, be realistic about the price that your property will achieve (see pages 187–8).

In areas such as West Lothian and Dunbartonshire, Fife, Dundee and Edinburgh, sales have done well year on year. According to the Council of Mortgage Lenders in 2012, 42 per cent of buyers bought for the first time, which is similar to the rest of the UK. Because of the different system of buying and selling, the process is generally faster than south of the border.

Most property is sold through solicitors rather than estate agents. Groups of local solicitors often market properties for sale through a separate business called a '**property centre**', where all enquiries are passed on to the relevant solicitor. The property centres charge about £200 to £250 for this service, which runs for up to six months. Solicitors offer the same full marketing

---

 The Scottish Solicitors Property Centre website (**www.sspc.co.uk**) features properties for sale across Scotland. Alternatively, go to the regional property centres such as **www.gspc.co.uk** and **www.espc.co.uk**, which also have fortnightly property guides.

service as estate agents. They also produce their own property guide papers, called the *GSPC Property Guide* and *ESPC Guide*, which are fortnightly, full-colour listings of properties on the market, available at all property centres and many shops throughout Scotland.

Estate agents charge commission, which will be from 1 per cent of the selling price. Solicitors also work on commission and, in addition, will charge for the legal work involved, although it is quite common for them to set a single percentage fee for both of these services. Get several quotations from solicitors and estate agents so that you can make a comparison. Choose one who is a member of a professional association, and see the general advice on choosing estate agents and solicitors on pages 95–102 and 108, and in particular on reading the contracts carefully before agreeing to them (see pages 100–2).

Jargon buster

Entry date The same as a completion date in England and Wales.
Fixed price A more definite price than the guideline price, which allows the possibility of a faster sale.
Guideline price Guide for buyers on which offers are based. Also known as the 'upset price'.
Property centre A group of solicitors who market properties for sale.

Setting a price

Your agent or solicitor will help you to decide the price, but also read the advice on researching your local market on pages 79–82. This is particularly important in a market such as Scotland where prices can vary dramatically and there are regional variations: different sectors can behave very differently, with some remaining static and others seeing significant uplift. To help you set a guideline price, the system in Scotland changed in December 2008 as anyone wishing to market a property for sale had to purchase a Home Report, which is based on the now scrapped Home Information Packs (HIPs) used in England and Wales. But, unlike the HIPs, the Home Report includes a survey and valuation of the property. This information is available to all buyers from the day the property is marketed.

BE CAREFUL!
Check out what prices properties have sold for in your street or area. For help, visit www.ros.gov.uk and www.housepricescotland.com.

Professional associations for estate agents and solicitors include the National Association of Estate Agents (**www.naea.co.uk**), the Property Ombudsman (**www.tpos.co.uk**) and the Law Society of Scotland (**www.lawscot.org.uk**).

BE CAREFUL!
When choosing a company to carry out a Home Report, it is important to ensure they are on as many lenders' panels as possible so that the buyer doesn't have to get another report, which can waste time and money.

The Home Report

The Home Report has made a massive difference to the Scottish buying and selling process as it offers a survey and valuation of the property upfront for buyers. This is because sellers now pay the cost of the report rather than lots of buyers having to have surveys carried out on the property to work out how much to bid for it. Prices for the report vary from £100 to £1,200, depending on the value of your property, but do shop around.

The report also includes an Energy Report (EPC, see pages 105–7) and a useful property questionnaire, which answers questions such as how long you, the seller, have owned the property, what Council Band applies to the property, and any other things that have happened during your property ownership, such as new windows or if your home has suffered from flooding.

Your representative will set a time and date by which sealed bids must be made, usually noon on a weekday, known as the '**closing date**'. The bids will set a price and suggest an **entry date**, which is the same as a completion date. When you receive this, read it carefully and discuss it with your adviser: the best price may not be the best bid. For example, a lower offer from a cash buyer or someone who wants an early completion date may be better.

Once you accept an offer you have a binding contract: if one of you changes your mind, you will have to pay compensation to the other. So you don't need to worry about whether your buyer has their finances in place.

In a hurry?
If you need to move very quickly, or if your property has not attracted much interest, you could offer it at a fixed price. This allows you to market the property and accept the first offer you are happy with, which may be at that price or possibly below.

For more information about Home Reports visit **www.scotland.gov.uk/Topics/Built-Environment/Housing/BuyingSelling/Home-Report** and for Scottish house prices visit **www.housepricesscotland.com** and **www.ros.gov.uk**.

Buying in Scotland

It is just as important to be organised when buying property in Scotland as in any other part of the country. But bear in mind other matters.

The key differences when buying in Scotland as opposed to England or Wales are summarised below.

- **Properties are priced** at a guide level of the lowest acceptable price, and offers are on the valuation price or, if the property is very popular, up to 30 per cent more.
- **Buyers** no longer always have to have surveys carried out; instead they can read the seller's Home Report.
- **You need to have** your finances for the property organised prior to making an offer – i.e. a mortgage offer from a company.
- **Offers are typically** made 'blind' to a deadline – so you can't negotiate on price, and you need to be sure you can afford your offer. However, sometimes you can make an offer and have it accepted without going to a closing date.
- **Once an offer** has been accepted, you are committed to the purchase and will have to pay compensation if you pull out.
- **A moving date** is set once the offer is agreed, so there are fewer problems with managing chains.
- **Property is sold** on an owner-occupier basis: there is no **freehold** and very little **leasehold** in Scotland.

Buying a property in Scotland has been made easier since the credit crunch (apart from the difficulty of getting a mortgage) thanks to the new Home Report, which the seller pays for, but you gain the benefit of a survey, EPC and information about the property (see page 188).

Start by reading the advice on pages 24–35 on working out what you can realistically afford. This is particularly important when buying in Scotland because if you make a successful bid but then can't raise the finance for it, you can be landed with a substantial demand for compensation. So do your figures, talk to a lender and get your MAP (see pages 40–1). If you are also selling a property, get as far along the path with it as you can – being able to offer quick completion can be the difference between success and failure in the Scottish market.

'If you are also selling a property in the Scottish market, being able to offer quick completion can be the difference between success and failure.'

Stamp collecting

Include SDLT in your calculations of what you can afford. The rates in Scotland are as follows. Up to £125,000 incurs no SDLT (up to £250,000 if you are a first time buyer).

Over £125,000 to £250,000	1 per cent
Over £250,000 to £500,000	3 per cent
Over £500,000 to £1 million	4 per cent
Over £1 million to £2 million	5 per cent
Over £2 million	7 per cent

There is also a fee for registering the title, charged on a sliding scale according to the price of the property you purchase.

Call your lawyer

It is important to choose your solicitor before looking at homes. This will enable you to make an offer on a property with a tight deadline. Personal recommendation is one of the best ways to choose, but make sure your solicitor has experience in dealing with properties in the area and of the type that you are buying. You can also visit the Scottish Law Society at www.lawscot.org.uk to find suitable firms. If you are buying from outside Scotland, you will still need a Scottish solicitor.

As with any other service, find out what the costs and terms are – for example, if the fee includes Stamp Duty Land Tax, registration fees, expenses and VAT.

Looking at properties

Once you have identified the likely areas where your preferred types of property exist (see pages 133–4), you can start looking at properties in your price range.

The guideline price of properties on the market is geared to stimulate interest, and successful bids are likely to be either around valuation or higher in a rising market. So do have a look at properties at a guideline price below your range: they may turn out to be just what you want.

Some sellers looking for a quick sale may put their property on at a 'fixed price' which is more like the asking price in England and Wales (see the box on page 188), and new build properties are also priced in this way.

Most solicitors' property centres and estate agents advertise in their own free newspaper and on websites. Some useful ones include: **www.aspc.co.uk** (Aberdeen); **www.espc.co.uk** (Edinburgh); **www.gspc.co.uk** (Glasgow) and **www.s1homes.com**. You can also search on **www.rightmove.co.uk**.

Home reports

These are incredibly useful reports for you to read prior to considering making an offer on a property as they give lots of useful information about the property, its condition, work required and – with the EPC (see pages 105–7) – how much your utility bills are likely to be. The property questionnaire furnishes you with details of changes the owner has made to the property, the council band the property is in and which company currently supplies the heating.

The report also gives an estimated price of what the property is worth in its current condition and what it would cost to re-build the property should it be damaged, which allows you to work out in advance what your buildings insurance cost would be.

The report not only contains this essential information, but will also help you secure a mortgage. Most lenders accept the survey and valuation in the Home Report, but some don't accept the valuation if the Home Report is more than 90 days old from the date of the property inspection as they feel the value may well have changed during this time. If a revised report is

Case study Mr and Mrs Sim

Mr and Mrs Sim currently live in a semi-detached property, which they had substantially extended two years ago. They were in a dillema about taking the next step up the property ladder. The four-bedroomed detached properties in the area they liked offered little extra space (sometimes even offered less!), but they were keen to increase their property 'ownership'.

As luck would have it, the house next door became vacant when their neighbours relocated to England and after letting it out for 12 months, the previous owners mentioned that they intended to sell.

Having played around with the idea of buy to let for a few months previously, Mr and Mrs Sim saw this as the perfect opportunity to take the next step. They negotiated a private purchase with their ex-neighbours, which went through extremely smoothly in about six weeks.

Despite one lender expressing concern about lending on the semi next door to their own house (because they feared the Sims would 'break through' to create one large detached property), Mr and Mrs Sim had managed to arrange the finance, organise a survey and successfully bid on the property.

So although they didn't get more space, they got a good investment in buy to let and will always ensure they keep good neighbours next door. The whole process was smooth, partly because of the system in Scotland where once an offer is accepted this means that you also exchange simultaneously.

'Most lenders accept the valuation in the Home Report unless it is more than 90 days old as they feel the value may have changed in this time.'

required, the same inspector would normally carry out the inspection and this would cost between £75 and £100. Other lenders are not keen on using valuations and reports from surveyors that are not on the 'panel' they usually choose from.

Making an offer

This is the really tricky bit because you only get one shot at it. The Home Report survey will give you an idea of the property's condition and what work is required as well as its estimated value. You may be able to make an offer straight away: ask your solicitor to contact his or her counterpart to find out if you can. If not, they should 'note' your interest. This means that if another party expresses interest in the property you can be kept informed of this. A closing date is likely to be fixed for the bids, but this is not guaranteed: it is quite common for vendors to accept offers and agree the deal ahead of the closing date.

Offers are made as sealed bids and the vital information is the price offered and the suggested entry date, when you complete the purchase – sometimes this can be weeks but it is usually a few months ahead. Discuss this date with your solicitor, taking into consideration the progress of the sale of your own property. A seller may accept a lower bid if the transaction can

---

Factors to consider when making an offer in Scotland

- What price did the surveyor value it at?
- What did similar properties sell for?
- Is there potential for extending or other changes that would add value?
- What fixtures and fittings are included?
- Is the local market rising, falling or static?
- Can you afford to offer more if you want to?
- If you are a cash buyer or have sold your property already, you will be more attractive to the vendor.
- What 'entry date' would suit the vendor best?
- Can you bear to go through all this again if your bid is rejected?

be completed quickly – and reject a higher bid that will take too long. If your bid is rejected, all you can do is put it down to experience and pick up the property papers again – but do ask why you weren't successful as you may get some useful feedback.

When a bid is successful

When a bid is accepted, the two solicitors negotiate the details of the contract, such as the fixtures and fittings (see page 111), and the date of completion. The letters between them are known as 'missives', and the equivalent of exchanging contracts in the English system is called '**concluding the missives**' in Scotland. At this point you will need to arrange building insurance on the property, but the seller continues their insurance too until the date of settlement. The solicitor also checks the title and reports on an exact description of the property and any conditions that you must understand as the new owner. After that, the solicitor does the conveyancing and prepares

> **Jargon buster**
> **Concluding the missives** Scottish term for exchanging contracts.
> **Disposition** Document transferring ownership.

the '**disposition**': a document transferring ownership to you.

The setting of a moving-in date makes the property chain less prone to delays than in England and Wales, as everybody is working to an agreed, binding schedule. However if you are moving to Scotland from another country you will have two sets of solicitors and it is important to keep up communication with all parties. About two weeks before the entry date you will be asked to provide the money for the deposit, stamp duty and your solicitor's fees. Your lender should transfer the balance of the money one day ahead of the entry date. The legal documents are typically signed either a few weeks before or just before the date of entry.

> '**The setting of a moving-in date in Scotland makes the property chain less prone to delays than in England and Wales, as everybody is working to an agreed, binding schedule.**'

Help for those on low incomes

There are a number of schemes to help those on low incomes in Scotland to buy property. Right to buy has been replaced by two new schemes, but there is also shared ownership.

Right to buy (RTB)

The RTB, which allows council and housing association tenants to purchase their home at a discount, has been suspended in many areas.

In 2012, a bill was passed to end the RTB for new tenants and on any new social housing supply. Over the last 30 years, over half a million homes have been sold at a discount and there are plans to build more homes for the social sector. To see if you are still eligible for the RTB, check with your landlord (usually the local authority or housing association).

- **Low-cost initiative for First-time Buyers (LIFT)** is the Scottish equivalent of England and Wales's HomeBuy scheme and helps people on low incomes to take a shared equity stake in a home.
- **Open market shared equity scheme** is run under LIFT and is similar to shared equity. It helps first-time buyers and people in the armed forces or those living under exceptional circumstances, such as you or a member of your family incurring a disability and needing to move. The scheme is also open to social tenants who don't have a right to buy their own property but would like to part buy a property on the open market.

For more information, read the latest booklet on open market shared equity schemes, which you can find via www.scotland.gov.uk/Topics/Built-Environment/Housing/BuyingSelling/lift.

Shared ownership

This allows you to buy a 25, 50 or 75 per cent share in a house or flat owned by a housing association, usually a new-build development. You can increase your share until it is owned outright. It is offered by many housing associations and some private developers. Council and housing association tenants are given priority.

For the Scottish Federation of Housing Associations, visit **www.sfha.co.uk**; for housing advice, visit **http://scotland.shelter.org.uk/**, and go to **www.scotland.gov.uk/Topics/Built-Environment/Housing** for shared equity schemes.

Selling and buying in Northern Ireland and Ireland

10

There are a number of differences between buying properties in England or Wales and Northern Ireland. If you are dealing south of the border in Ireland, the process and terms used are different again. This chapter puts you on the right track.

Selling and buying in Northern Ireland

Like the rest of the UK, Northern Ireland suffered price falls in 2007. Unfortunately, prices typically fell further (over 50 per cent) than the rest of the UK as prices rose to an average of £199,000 and at their lowest dropped to £93,000.

In the first quarter of 2012, average prices, according to NISRA, were at a low of £93,000. However, property price changes are increasingly different by region, so it is important to check out what is happening in the local markets before you decide whether to buy or sell.

Whose land is it anyway?

There is a long history of confusion about ground rent on properties in Northern Ireland. In some cases, several people can claim to be due ground rent on the same land. To deal with this, purchasers of a property must now redeem any ground rent on it, turning it into a freehold, before they can register ownership with the Land Registry. This legislation does not apply to flats. Your solicitor should be able to advise if this must be done. The cost for compulsory purchase is nine times the annual ground rent, paid as compensation to the freeholder, plus a fee to the Land Registry office and a fee to your solicitor for witnessing the statutory form GR1, obtainable from the Land Registers of Northern Ireland (www.landwebni.gov.uk). A leaflet explaining the Ground Rents Acts is available on the Office of Law Reform website at www.dfpni.gov.uk/index/laws-and-regulations/law-reform.htm.

Selling in Northern Ireland

The process of selling property in Northern Ireland is the same as in England and Wales, especially now Home Information Packs have been dropped as these were never introduced in Northern Ireland.

Buying in Northern Ireland

If you are buying property in Northern Ireland, the following areas differ from buying in England and Wales.

Stamp Duty Land Tax (SDLT)

The rates of stamp duty are the same as for England and Wales (see page 22), but SDLT has been waived

For advice on housing, go to **www.shelter.org.uk**; **www.nihe.gov.uk** (the Northern Ireland Housing Executive) and **www.co-ownership.org** (NICHA, the regional body for shared ownership). To track property prices in Northern Ireland, go to **www.nisra.gov.uk/housepriceindex/HPI.html**.

in certain areas on properties selling for less than £150,000 in a government bid to encourage property development. However, you will still need to provide the SDLT return form for the property to be registered (see page 177).

Buying on a low income

There are a number of schemes to help buyers on a low income.

- **Co-ownership:** The Northern Ireland Co-ownership Housing Association (NICHA) is Northern Ireland's body for shared ownership where you part own, part rent the home. There are sometimes limits on the number of applications that can be made per month. The properties available are set within certain value limits by local councils and are capped at £175,000. They do not include housing executive or housing association residences. You can apply direct to the NICHA or through an estate agent. You can purchase 50–90 per cent of the property, although you can also increase the share of ownership in portions of 5 per cent at a time. There are set costs for purchasing via this scheme, which include buying necessary legal work and a valuation. You

should be prepared to budget for £350–£400.

- **Right to buy:** Tenants of a local authority, a housing association or housing executive are usually permitted to buy their home after living in it for five years and a discount will be applied to the purchase price. Up to four people can buy together if they have been living there for 12 months and it may be possible to buy part of your home as this scheme has been extended to include equity sharing. This is called the Statutory House Sales Scheme.

Estate agents

As in the rest of the UK, all estate agents need to belong to one of the two redress schemes (see pages 97–100). However, this doesn't require any particular specialist education unless the agent is a member of the Royal Institution of Chartered Surveyors (RICS) as surveyors have to have a degree and further education to qualify in their profession. This means that all agents now have to adhere to the redress organisation's code of conduct (see page 99), so if you have a problem, you have an independent third party to refer your complaint to. Fees are

---

Northern Ireland property search websites include **www.findaproperty.com**, **www.nidirect.gov.uk/low-cost-home-ownership-schemes**, **www.propertynews.com**, **www.propertypal.com** and **www.rightmove.co.uk**. See also using property price surveys on pages 75–9.

negotiable, but the typical rate is 1.5 per cent of the selling price. When market conditions are poor, you may have to pay upfront for advertising. See pages 95–101 for advice on selecting an agent.

The legal side

Only solicitors can carry out conveyancing in Northern Ireland. Fees vary widely and it is a competitive market. Some firms stick to a charge of 1 per cent of the selling price plus an hourly rate (all plus VAT), others have a different fee structure. Ask for a written estimate of their costs, including tax, registration, search and other expenses, so that you can make a proper comparison.

Most property sales are by 'private treaty' (see page 200) and some go to auction (see page 204). There are also cases of buyers being invited to tender for a property in a sealed bid, as in Scotland (see page 188).

Energy performance

Energy performance certificates (EPCs) were introduced on 30 June 2008 for larger buildings in Northern Ireland. All new builds must have an EPC from September 2008 and all property sales and rentals must one by the end of 2008. For further information visit www.dfpni.gov.uk/energy-performance-of-buildings.

Get it surveyed

All properties, new and old, should have an independent survey of the property (see pages 153–4).

New build

The average price of a newly built home in Northern Ireland is, according to the National House Building Council, about £138,500. There are several guarantee schemes run by developers of new properties, including those run by the Construction Employers Federation (www.cefni.co.uk), the National House Building Council (NHBC) (www.nhbc.co.uk) and the Construction Register Ltd. For full contact details see Useful addresses on pages 209–15.

The Home Charter Scheme

The Law Society of Northern Ireland operates a compulsory kitemark quality scheme for solicitors. It sets minimum standards for typical tasks, providing a benchmark against which complaints can be measured. Go to www.lawsoc-ni.org for more information.

For more information on new builds in Northern Ireland read the 'Northern Ireland Housing Bulletin' at **www.dsdni.gov.uk/housing_bulletins**.

Selling and buying in Ireland

The Irish property market witnessed a tremendous boom up until 2006, but since then the property market has slumped. Trying to sell a home is tough, as is the decision whether to buy or continue renting.

The property market in Ireland has had a disastrous few years. Property prices grew from around €75,000 in 1996 to a peak of €311,000 in late in 2006. Although different price indices show different numbers, most agree with the Daft.ie second quarter of 2012 report that prices have fallen so far in Ireland by around 50 per cent. Dublin, as well as other areas, were hit hard with prices falling from 50 to 60 per cent. Reports for 2012 so far suggest prices in areas like Dublin are stabilising.

Just as in the rest of the UK, though, these price falls vary across the regions and are property type specific. Family homes appear to have held their value better than most properties. In some areas, apartments have fallen in value by 50 per cent, and in other areas where there is a shortage of supply they are selling quite well.

> **'Trying to sell your property in a falling and uncertain market is very hard – setting a reasonable price is difficult.'**

Selling in ireland

Trying to sell your property in a falling and uncertain market is very hard. Properties are starting to sell in Ireland, but only if priced competitively. A real difficulty is setting the price correctly from the start. With none too many properties being sold, agents have got few, if any, comparables.

Research prices by choosing sales agents that are selling property in your area. Take their advice,

See pages 119 and 155 for advice on how to plan for buying and selling in a falling or a strong market. For the latest house price information visit the Central Statistics Office at **http://www.cso.ie** and search for the Residential Property Price Index or see also **www.daft.ie/report/**.

however hard it may be to hear that your property isn't worth as much as you thought. If you get the price wrong at the start, your property is unlikely to sell, but price it competitively and you could get a sale within 10–15 weeks, or even have buyers competing.

If you price right and your property is in good condition, it should sell reasonably quickly. To help reduce delays, appoint a legal firm early on so they can collect your title deeds. Estate agents in

Ireland are often referred to as auctioneers and have to hold either an Auctioneer's Licence or a House Agent's Licence. Their members must follow set auction procedures. They will set an advised minimum value (AMV), but in a falling market, be prepared to deal with low offers.

Negative equity

Due to the price falls, some people have to sell their home for less than they paid for it. This is a tricky situation to be in and it is important to consider what other options there are. For example, you may be able to rent a room to help pay the mortgage (you can earn up to €10,000 tax free) or rent out the entire property and wait for prices to turn the corner. Talk to your lender about your circumstances as they are obliged to help you through these difficult times and see what help you can secure to either continue paying your mortgage or, if you need to sell up, whether you can take your loan with you. In addition, seek independent financial advice as you may still be able to move home if required with the help of newly approved negative equity mortgages. There are also schemes such as the Mortgage Interest Supplement, which, if you are eligible, can help you with your existing payments. Visit www.citizensinformation.ie for more information.

Selling by private treaty

This is a contract that commits both parties to the sale. Your buyer will lose the deposit if they withdraw from the deal. Obviously you have to be totally committed to selling your home before signing it.

Buying in Ireland

The good news for new buyers in the Irish property market is that there is plenty of stock to choose from and although some of the incentive schemes and grants to first-time buyers have been stopped, prices have fallen back so much they are making buying affordable

 To get the most up-to-date information on sterling–euro conversions, see the website **www.xe.com**. It is worth checking the conversion rate regularly as markets fluctuate all the time.

again. Mortgage costs have fallen to around 12 per cent of net income for an average first-time couple and first-time buyers now account for 45 per cent of new mortgages issued.

The two key difficulties for new buyers, particularly first-time buyers, are whether to buy or continue renting, particularly as rents are starting to rise versus property prices, and – second – to understand what's happening in the market. To help, see page 15, which explains what you need to consider, and pages 74–5 of Understanding your local market. In addition, it is important to keep an eye on the new build market and stamp duty charges as first-time buyers are currently still exempt from paying taxes when buying a property. However, there are now two other charges for homeowners. The first is an annual Household Charge of €100, which goes towards funding local services. The second is an additional annual Non-principal Private Residence Charge (NPPR) on residential properties that are not your only or main residence on 31 March of any year. The charge is €200 per year, per property. There are exemptions including if you are moving home, have a granny flat, moving into a nursing home or are separating/divorcing. The payment needs to be received by 30 June each year or a late fee applies.

Stamp Duty Tax

Stamp Duty Tax in Ireland was simplified in December 2010. This has led to a major change to many exemptions from the previous Stamp Duty Tax rules, including:

- No exemptions on properties valued under €127,500
- No additional relief for first-time buyers

If you had or transferred a property from a close relative, you used to pay half the normal Stamp Duty Tax rate. This was abolished in December 2010 on residential properties, and for those who used to be able to transfer land with no Stamp Duty Tax, this is now applied. In 2014, this change in the rules will also apply to non-residential properties.

Current Stamp Duty Tax rates

For property values up to €1 million the rate is 1 per cent and for any balance over the million, it is 2 per cent.

As these rules have been changed and can vary by year, it is worth seeking advice to find out the Stamp Duty implications of purchasing a home.

Keep up to date with stamp duty changes via www.citizensinformation.ie.

 The contact details for the Law Society of Ireland are: **www.lawsociety.ie** or telephone 03531 672 4800. Through the Law Society you will be able to contact reputable firms with which to deal.

Mortgage interest relief

First-time buyers do get mortgage interest relief. The relief is applied to the mortgage payments by the lender and you get 25 per cent for the first two years. If you aren't a first time buyer, the relief is at a rate of 15 per cent from 2012 until 2017.

Further special rates can apply, so make sure you talk to your lender, especially if you bought your property between 2004 and 2008.

Financing a purchase with a mortgage

As always, the first step is to decide what you can genuinely afford (see the guidance on pages 24–35). Remember to include the 'hidden costs' such as stamp duty (see box on page 201) and legal fees.

Land Registry fees are charged on a scale from €125 to €625 depending on the property price. Total legal fees are likely to be 1–2 per cent of the purchase price. These fees are negotiable and it could pay to shop around among recommended firms. Always use a member of the Law Society of Ireland (see box, overleaf). Deposits of 8 per cent or more of the selling price are also usually required. The typical loan term was 20 years, but since the start of the recession this now varies.

Low income support

There are a number of schemes in Ireland designed to help those on low incomes onto the property ladder.

- **Rent-a-Room scheme:** This is a government-run scheme allowing owner occupiers to rent out a spare room for up to €10,000 a year free of tax. You'll need to tell your mortgage company you intend to do this. This scheme could give your finances the kick-start they need, and, of course, you'll need to look for properties with at least two bedrooms.

- **Affordable housing schemes:** There are some ways you can get help onto the property ladder, but due to the economic climate it is limited. The shared ownership scheme, for example, has been stopped. Here we explain some of the ways you can still get help on the property ladder.

- **Incremental Purchase Scheme:** This scheme only helps those renting or waiting for social housing. It is only for new build properties and discounts of 40–60 per cent can be applied.

- **The Mortgage Allowance Scheme:** This is for tenants of local authorities or housing associations. It offers up to

> **'Decide what you can genuinely afford, bearing in mind stamp duty and legal fees. They add up quickly.'**

€11,500 to reduce your mortgage payments during the first five years of the loan.

Buying a home
See the advice on pages 124–45 on deciding what you need and want, researching the local market and choosing what to view. Estate agents in Ireland will tell you the advised minimum value (AMV) of properties. This is like the asking price in Northern Ireland (see pages 199–200) and has superseded guide prices. Beware, though, that in a tough market properties can be sold at 20 per cent less than the asking price, so talk to as many agents as you can before making an offer.

New builds
Up until 2006 there was a massive boom in new homes, partly fuelled by the non-imposition of stamp duty on new properties under 125 square metres (see page 201). Since the downturn, new build completions have plummeted from 93,500 in 2006 to under 10,000 in 2011 and a similar number are expected for 2012.

Due to financial problems and potential cost cutting, a snagging survey is a MUST to ensure that the property meets the highest standards in construction and finishing. Make sure that the

New home, new problems?
New homes are notorious for the number of 'snagging' problems lurking behind that new brickwork (see page 130). In Ireland, one of the main guarantee schemes is operated by Construction Register Limited (www.c-r-l.com) that offers homebuyers a ten-year warranty covering structural flaws. There is also a scheme run by the National House Building Council (NHBC) (www.nhbc.co.uk). You can also request an Architects Certificate, which is not a warranty but states that the property has been built according to their standards. While this is better than nothing, it is still important to have new homes checked by an independent snagging company (see page 156).

snagging survey is carried out prior to exchange.

Timber-framed (as opposed to cavity block construction) houses have become more popular, partly because they are quicker to build. Read the advice on buying newly built properties on pages 127–9, and see the box on page 203 for information on guarantees.

Prior to 2008, the fast pace of the market led to many new-build houses being sold ahead of construction on the strength of the brochure. While this can give you more say on customising the house to your requirements (for example, placement of lighting and sockets and style of decoration), there is a risk of the project overrunning

Irish estate agent professional bodies are the The Society of Chartered Surveyors Ireland (**www.scsi.ie**), and the Institute of Professional Auctioneers and Valuers (**www.ipav.ie**). The professional body for chartered surveyors in Ireland is the Society of Chartered Surveyors (**www.scsi.ie**).

Freehold or leasehold?

Property in Ireland can be freehold or leasehold. However, most leaseholders have the right to buy the freehold title, which is worth doing as it makes the legal position more straightforward and therefore the property is easier to sell.

and the house not being completed in time – which can be a massive problem if you are part of a chain. Negotiate a moving-in date at the time you agree a deal.

Contract or auction?

Over 10 per cent of Irish properties are sold at auction. This is always a risky business as you have to check out the property (at no little expense) in advance and then you can get sucked into bidding more than you wanted to at the auction before the gavel falls and you are faced with a demand for the deposit (see the advice on buying through auctions on page 137). However, the auction proccess is much quicker than buying or selling on the open market as deals done on the day are concluded within the month. The introduction of AMVs has tried to ensure that properties are priced nearer to the actual selling price.

Do get your legal firm to check the contract for the property in advance, and do have a survey undertaken if you are serious about buying. Remember also that vendors are often happy to consider offers made ahead of the auction, which can save a lot of heartache and hassle for both parties.

Most property in Ireland is sold by 'private treaty' (the equivalent of a contract that goes to exchange and completion in England and Wales) with a 'contract for sale' being signed after a price has been agreed. A deposit (usually 10 per cent of the selling price) is paid when this is signed, and can be lost if you pull out. The contract sets a completion date on which the balance must be paid. Legal queries are dealt with in the intervening period, which can be a slow business and is why there is a great potential for gazumping in Ireland (see page 160).

One important check for a family residence property is that there is a declaration of consent from both spouses, which prevents one from selling the home without the agreement of the other.

Get a survey done

There is no HIP system proposed for Ireland, and as with all purchases, the message is 'buyer beware'. You should commission your own independent survey of the property to check for any flaws. The survey often pays for itself in financial terms as it can lead to re-negotiation of the price to allow for repairs, but it can also provide peace of mind: you know what you are buying. Do not rely on your lender's valuation-only survey: there is advice on the other two types of survey on pages 153–4. Surveys cost around 300 to over 1,000.

Glossary

AMV Advised minimum value, the phrase for the lowest acceptable price in Ireland.

APR Annual percentage rate, the figure that shows the true cost of the loan (or mortgage).

Asking price Price at which a property is marketed.

Balance outstanding The amount of a loan still owed.

Base rate Interest rate set by the Bank of England, which is the rate at which banks can borrow money from the Bank of England, and is therefore what the banks use to set their interest rates.

Bridging loan A loan allowing you to buy a property before finalising the sale of another property.

Building regulations Standards of build set for new buildings, extensions and renovations.

Buildings insurance The insurance on the structure of a property.

Buy to let Purchasing a property to rent out to tenants.

Buying off plan Purchasing an un-built property from the plans.

BBR Bank of England base rate (see above).

Capital The initial mortgage loan.

Capital Gains Tax Tax on profit from selling certain assets, not including your main place of residence.

CH Central heating.

Chain A series of people linked by related property sales and purchases.

Commission A fee based on a percentage of the selling or purchase price; can apply to an independent financial adviser as well as an estate agent.

Commonhold A recently introduced form of tenure offering an alternative to leasehold agreements.

Completion The final part of the transaction when the transfer of the property title is legally given to the new owner.

Condition report This complements a mortgage valuation to assess the property's overall condition.

Conditions of sale The detailed standard terms governing the duties and rights of the buyer and seller.

Contract The agreement to sell or purchase.

Conveyancing The legal and administrative process of transferring ownership of land and/or property.

Covenant A promise in a deed to do (or not do) certain things.

Deeds The documents confirming ownership of property. Also known as title deeds.

Deposit The down payment on a property, paid when contracts are exchanged.

DG Double-glazing.

Disbursements Costs incurred during the conveyancing process, which will be charged to the client.

Early redemption Paying off a loan earlier than its term.

e-conveyancing Carrying out conveyancing through web and email as well as over the phone.

Endowment mortgage A loan where you only pay off the interest, linked to an endowment investment policy designed to pay off the sum borrowed at the end of the term.

Equity The difference between the price of a property sold and the loan on it.

Exchange of contracts A binding legal agreement that confirms the intention to transfer ownership of a property between a buyer and seller.

Final sale price The agreed price of a property that is finalised at the time of exchange.

Fixtures and fittings The term for the items attached to or part of a property, such as doors and light switches.

Freehold Ownership of a property and the land it is situated on.

FSA The Financial Services Authority (the Financial Conduct Authority (FCA) from 2013, see page 25).

Gazumping When another person's (higher) offer is accepted, after a lower offer has already been accepted, but not become legally binding (i.e. before exchange of contracts).

Gazundering When a purchaser reduces their offer at a late stage in the buying process, such as on the day of exchange.

GCH Gas central heating.

Ground rent Payment by the leaseholder to the freeholder. Low sums are sometimes referred to as a peppercorn rent.

Guide price The marketing price of a property in Scotland, usually lower than the final price.

Higher lending charge Policy taken out by the lender (but usually paid for by you) to cover them if the borrower does not make payments.

Home Report Purchaser's Information Pack, mandatory in Scotland from 2008.

IFA Independent financial adviser.

Indemnity policy Insurance to protect a property owner in a dispute over ownership or restrictive covenants.

Instruction Telling an agent you want them to sell your property.

Interest-only mortgage A loan where you only pay the interest on the amount borrowed over the term of the mortgage.

Intermediary A finance company offering products from a number of providers.

Joint agency When two agents are instructed.

Joint tenancy When two people own a property together and if one dies, the property automatically passes to the other, irrespective of the will.

Land certificate Certificate confirming ownership of a property, issued by the Land Registry.

Leasehold Ownership for a set period, which is most commonly applied to flats and other shared buildings.

Licensed conveyancer A specialist trained in transfer of property ownership.

Local searches Information on planning and environmental matters obtained from the local authority.

Mortgage A loan for which property is the collateral.

Mortgage Agreement in Principle (MAP) An outline agreement to provide a loan to a specified person.

Mortgage protection policy Life insurance taken out by the borrower so that the loan is paid off if they die or are sick (although policies do vary).

Mortgage redemption penalty The charge sometimes made by the lender if you pay off your mortgage early.

Mortgage roll number or reference number The reference number identifying your loan

to the lender, required to draw down your title deeds when selling.

Multiple agency When you instruct more than two estate agencies.

Negative equity When your mortgage loan is higher on the property than the price you could sell it for.

Office copy The 'official' copy of an entry from the Land Registry.

Part exchange An arrangement in which your current home is bought by a developer (or a company they outsource to) to free up your monies to purchase their home.

Planning permission The go-ahead from a local authority for large physical changes to a property, such as adding a porch or garage.

Property portal Websites with properties from a variety of agents.

PVC Plasticised polyvinyl chloride, the material used to make plastic window frames.

Repayment mortgage Loan where you pay the interest and the sum borrowed off at the same time for an agreed period.

Restrictive covenant Legal restriction on what can be done on a property or on land.

Retention The withholding of part of a loan until structural faults are corrected.

Sales particulars The information prepared to market a property.

SDG Secondary double-glazing.

Sealed bid Making an offer in a sealed envelope by a set date and time.

Searches See local searches.

Shared equity This is where you purchase a percentage of the property and can wait five or more years before you buy the rest of the property.

Shared ownership Scheme where a housing association helps in the purchase of a property.

Snagging The process of spotting the defects on new building work.

Sole agency When you only instruct one estate agent.

Stamp Duty Land Tax (SDLT) Tax paid when you buy property, calculated as a percentage of the price.

Subject to contract When a sale has been agreed but contracts have not been exchanged. Using the phrase prevents an offer being interpreted as a binding agreement.

Subject to survey An offer made with the proviso that it may be amended or withdrawn if the survey shows flaws in the property.

Sum insured The insured amount that will be paid in the event of a valid claim being made.

Surrender value The amount received if a life insurance policy is terminated early.

Survey A report on the condition of a property.

Tenants in common When more than one person owns a property but each person's share forms part of their estate if they die.

Term insurance A life insurance policy with a time limit, usually used to cover the length of a mortgage.

Tied agent An agent who also represents a limited list of financial companies or is owned by a financial company.

Title deeds The documents proving ownership of land.

Top-up mortgage An additional mortgage when the first loan is not sufficient for your needs.

Under offer The stage between having an offer accepted and exchanging contracts.

UPVC Unplasticised polyvinyl chloride, the material used to make windowframes.

Vacant possession When a property being sold has no one living in it.

Valuation The price a mortgage lender thinks a property will sell for. A mortgage valuation is a check by the lender that the property is as described in your mortgage application and that if you default on payment, the mortgage company will be able to get their money back when they sell your property.

Variable rate When the interest rate is not fixed and can go up or down.

Vendor The seller.

Useful addresses

Association of British Insurers
51 Gresham Street
London EC2V 7HQ
Tel: 020 7600 3333
www.abi.org.uk

British Association of Removers (BAR)
Tangent House
62 Exchange Road
Watford
Hertfordshire WD18 0TG
Tel: 01923 699480
www.bar.co.uk

The British Holiday & Home Parks Association
Chichester House
6 Pullman Court
Great Western Road
Gloucester GL1 3ND
Tel: none available
www.ukparks.com

Building Cost Information Service (BCIS)
12 Great George Street
London SW1P 3AD
Tel: 020 7695 1500
www.bcis.co.uk

BuildStore Ltd
Unit 1, Kingsthorne Park
Nettlehill Road
Houstoun Industrial Estate
Livingston EH54 5DB
Tel: 0845 223 4888
www.buildstore.co.uk

Communities and Local Government
Eland House
Bressenden Place
London SW1E 5DU
Tel: 0303 444 0000
www.communities.gov.uk

Construction Employers Federation
143 Malone Road
Belfast BT9 6SU
Tel: 028 9087 7143
www.cefni.co.uk

Construction Register Ltd
2nd Floor
Rose Hose
Derryvolgie Avenue
Belfast
Northern Ireland BT9 6FL
Tel: 02890 667 899
http://structuralinsurance.com

Council for Licensed Conveyancers (CLC)
16 Glebe Road
Chelmsford
Essex CM1 1QG
Tel: 01245 349599
www.clc-uk.org

Council of Mortgage Lenders (CML)
Bush House
North West Wing
Aldwych
London WC2B 4PJ
Tel: 0845 373 6771
www.cml.org.uk

Designs on Property Ltd
Newland House
The Point
Weaver Road
Lincoln LN6 3QN
Tel: 0845 838 1763
www.designsonproperty.co.uk

Electrical Contractors' Association (ECA)
ESCA House
34 Palace Court
London W2 4HY
Tel: 020 7313 4800
www.eca.co.uk

English Heritage
1 Waterhouse Square
138-142 Holborn
London EC1N 2ST
Tel: 0870 333 1181
www.english-heritage.org.uk

Environment Agency
National Customer Contact Centre
PO Box 544
Rotherham S60 1BY
Tel: 03708 506 506
www.environment-agency.gov.uk.

ExCel London
One Western Gateway
Royal Victoria Dock
London E16 1XL
Tel: 020 7069 5000
www.excel-london.co.uk

Federation of Master Builders (FMB)
Gordon Fisher House
14–15 Great James Street
London WC1N 3DP
Tel: 020 7242 7583
www.fmb.org.uk

Financial Ombudsman Service (FOS)
South Quay Plaza
183 Marsh Wall
London E14 9SR
Tel: 08000 234 567
www.financialombudsman.org.uk

Financial Services Authority (FSA) (FCA from 2013, see page 25)
25 The North Colonnade
Canary Wharf
London E14 5HS
Tel: 020 7066 1000
www.fsa.gov.uk

Guarantee Protection Insurance Ltd (GPI)
37 Carrick Street, Ayr
South Ayrshire KA7 1NS
Tel: 01292 268 020
www.gp-insurance.co.uk/main.php

Health Protection Agency
151 Buckingham Palace Road
London SW1W 9SZ
Tel: 020 7811 7000
www.hpa.org.uk

Homecheck
Landmark Information Group
Legal and Financial, The Smith
Centre
The Fairmile
Henley-on-Thames RG9 6AB
Tel: 0844 844 9966
www.homecheck.co.uk

Hometrack Data Systems Ltd
Sixth Floor
The Chambers
Chelsea Harbour
London SW10 0XF
Tel: 0845 013 2350
www.hometrack.co.uk

**Homes and Communities
Agency**
To find your nearest HomeBuy
agent visit http://www.
homesandcommunities.co.uk/
homebuy_agents

The Independent Park Homes
Advisory Service
17 Ashley Wood Park
Tarrant Keyneston
Blandford Forum
Dorset DT11 9JJ
Tel: 01258 451838
www.iphas.co.uk

**Institute of Professional
Auctioneers and Valuers**
IPAV Headquarters
129 Lower Baggot Street
Dublin 2
Ireland
Tel: 003531 678 5685
www.ipav.ie

LABC Services
Third Floor
66 South Lambeth Road
London SW8 1RL
Tel: 020 7091 6860
www.labc.uk.com

**Law Society of England and
Wales**
The Law Society's Hall
113 Chancery Lane
London WC2A 1PL
Tel: 020 7242 1222
www.lawsociety.org.uk

Law Society of Ireland
Blackhall Place
Dublin 7
Ireland
Tel: 003531 672 4800
www.lawsociety.ie

Law Society of Northern Ireland
96 Victoria Street
Belfast BT1 3GN
Northern Ireland
Tel: 028 9023 1614
www.lawsoc-ni.org

Law Society of Scotland
26 Drumsheugh Gardens
Edinburgh EH3 7YR
Tel: 0131 226 7411
www.lawscot.org.uk

Legal Ombudsman
PO Box 6806
Wolverhampton WV1 9WJ
Tel: 0300 555 0333
www.legalombudsman.org.uk

The Listed Property Owners Club
Lower Dane
Hartlip
Kent ME9 7TE
Tel: 01795 844939
www.lpoc.co.uk

Lloyds Banking Group plc
33 Old Broad Street
London EC2N 1HZ
Tel: 020 7626 1500
www.lloydsbankinggroup.com

The NEC
Birmingham B40 1NT
Tel: 0121 780 4141
www.necgroup.co.uk

National Association of Estate Agents (NAEA)
Arbon House
6 Tournament Court
Edgehill Drive
Warwick CV34 6LG
Tel: 0844 387 0555
www.naea.co.uk

National Federation of Builders (NFB)
B & CE Building
Manor Royal
Crawley RH10 9QP
Tel: 0845 057 8160
www.builders.org.uk

National Guild of Removers and Storers
PO Box 690
Chesham
Buckinghamshire HP5 1WR
Tel: 01494 792279
www.ngrs.co.uk

The National House Building Council (NHBC)
NHBC House
Davy Avenue
Knowlhill
Milton Keynes MK5 8FP
Tel: 0844 633 1000
www.nhbc.co.uk

National Inspection Council for Electrical Installation Contracting (NICEIC)
Warwick House
Houghton Hall Park
Houghton Regis
Dunstable
Bedfordshire LU5 5ZX
Tel: 0870 013 0382
www.niceic.com

The National Park Homes Council
Catherine House
Victoria Road
Aldershot
Hants GU11 1SS
Tel: 01252 318251
www.theparkhome.net

New Home Advisor
100 South Street
Bishops Stortford
Herts CM23 3BG
Tel: 0844 409 7301
www.newhomeadvisor.co.uk

Northern Ireland Federation of Housing Associations
6c Citylink Business Park
Albert Street
Belfast BT12 4HB
Tel: 028 9023 0446
www.nifha.org

OneSearch Direct
1st Floor, Skypark SP1
8 Elliot Place
Glasgow G3 8EP
Tel: 08000 520 117
www.onesearchdirect.co.uk

Property Care Association (PCA)
Lakeview Court
Ermine Business Park
Huntingdon
Cambs PE29 6XR
Tel: 0844 375 4301
www.property-care.org

The Property Ombudsman
Milford House
43–55 Milford Street
Salisbury
Wiltshire SP1 2BP
Tel: 01722 333306
www.tpos.co.uk

Post Office Ltd
Customer Care
FREEPOST PO Box 740
Barnsley S73 0UF
Tel: 08457 22 33 44
www.postoffice.co.uk

The Removals Industry Ombudsman Scheme
PO Box 841
Chesham
Bucks HP5 9BB
Tel: 01494 785388
www.removalsombudsman.org.uk

Royal Institution of Chartered Surveyors (RICS)
Parliament Square
London SW1P 3AD
Tel: 0870 333 1600
www.rics.org

Scottish Federation of Housing Associations (SFHA)
3rd Floor
Sutherland House
149 St Vincent Street
Glasgow G2 5NW
Tel: 0141 332 8113
www.sfha.co.uk

Scottish Legal Complaints Commission
The Stamp Office
10-14 Waterloo Place
Edinburgh EH1 3EG
Tel: 0131 528 5111
www.scottishlegalcomplaints.org.uk

Shelter
88 Old Street
London EC1V 9HU
Tel: 0808 800 4444
www.shelter.org.uk

The Society of Chartered Surveyors Ireland
38 Merrion Square
Dublin 2
Ireland
Tel: 003531 644 5500
www.scsi.ie

UpMyStreet
111 Buckingham Palace Road
London SW1W 0SR
www.upmystreet.com

Which?
Castlemead
Gascoyne Way
Hertford SG14 1LH
Tel: 01992 822800
www.which.co.uk/switch
www.which.co.uk

Zurich Insurance
The Zurich Centre
3000 Parkway
Whiteley
Fareham
Hampshire PO15 7JZ
Tel: 08000 966 233
www.zurich.co.uk

Property-related websites
www.eigroup.co.uk
www.findaproperty.com
www.houseweb.co.uk
www.myhouseprice.com
www.nesltd.co.uk/find-an-assessor
www.ourproperty.co.uk
www.periodproperty.co.uk
www.primelocation.com
www.propertyauctionnews.co.uk
www.propertybroker.co.uk
www.propertynews.com (for Northern Ireland and Ireland)
www.propertypal.com (Northern Ireland property)

www.rightmove.co.uk
www.ruralpropertyindex.co.uk
www.ruralscene.co.uk
www.whichmortgageadvisers.co.uk
www.zoopla.co.uk

Websites dealing with property-related money issues

www.adrnow.org.uk (advice on alternative dispute resolution)
www.citizensadvice.org.uk (Citizens Advice Bureau – regional offices)
www.communitylegaladvice.org.uk (Community Legal Service)
www.co-ownership.org (regional body for shared ownership)
www.designsonproperty.co.uk
www.direct.gov.uk (directory of public services)
www.hmrc.gov.uk/sdlt/ (HM Revenue & Cutoms)
www.iammoving.com (change of address service)
www.landregistry.gov.uk (registers title to land in England and Wales)
www.lease-advice.org (Leasehold Advisory Service)
www.lloydsbankinggroup.com/media1/research/halifax_hpi.asp (Halifax house price index)
www.moneynet.co.uk (finance comparisons)
www.nationaldebtline.co.uk (advice on dealing with debt problems)
www.nationwide.co.uk/hpi (Nationwide house price index)
www.planningportal.gov.uk (online planning resource)
www.propertybroker.co.uk (service for buying and selling property)
www.scotland.gov.uk (Scottish government – advice on housing in Scotland)
www.tradingstandards.gov.uk (consumer protection information)
www.unbiased.co.uk (independent financial advice)

Index

accident, illness and unemployment
  insurance 49, 61
advertisements
  company notice boards 137
  estate agents 93–4
  'For Sale' signs 93, 95, 103
  newspapers 136
  notes through doors 137
  private advertisements 104
advised minimum value (AMV)
  (Ireland) 199–200, 204
affordability 24–35, 57
affordable home ownership schemes
  12, 12, 60
  Ireland 202
APR (annual percentage rate) 38
assets and liabilities 24–6
auction sales 137, 138
  Ireland 204

bankruptcy, mortgage applications
  and 33
banks
  electronic money transfer 48, 164
  mortgage loans 40, 51
bidding war 75
boundaries 110–11, 156
bridging loans 47
builders
  mortgage schemes 40, 128
  see also newly built houses
building regulations 92
building societies 37, 51
buildings and contents insurance
  64–70, 82, 92, 163
buying a property 19, 20, 123–55
  at auction 137, 138
  choosing a property type 124–6
  discounted property 138
  disputes with seller 183
  environmental risks 64, 65, 82, 148–9
  in a falling market 155
  fixtures and fittings 91, 145, 183

guarantees and safety certificates
  111, 149, 184
house-hunting 135–8
  in Ireland 200–205
  location 133–4, 147
  non-agent methods 136–8
  Northern Ireland 196–8
  renting before buying 119, 138, 156,
    159
  repossessed houses 138
  in Scotland 189–93
  in a strong market 155
  through an estate agent 135–6
  see also conveyancing; flats and
    apartments; newly built houses;
    offers; viewings

car 171
cash buyers 119, 155, 159
chain situation 13, 20, 113, 122, 138,
  156–64
  avoiding 159
  failed chains 160
  management 20–1, 159, 161–4
change of address notification 170,
  171, 172
children, moving with 173
completion 13, 101, 112, 113, 162,
  163–4
  balance of purchase price 164
  completion date 163, 164
conservation areas 150
contents insurance see buildings and
contents insurance
conveyancers see solicitors and
conveyancers
conveyancing 109–13
  buyer's questions 111
  chain situation 13, 20, 113, 122, 138,
    156–64
  completion 13, 101, 112, 162, 163–4
  contract of sale 111
  d-i-y conveyancing 110

delays 110, 122, 181
exchange of contracts 13, 28, 101,
    112, 162, 164
  Northern Ireland 198
  Scotland 193
County Court Judgements (CCJs)
    28, 32
credit record, poor 32, 59–60
crime issues 82
critical illness insurance (CIC) 49

damp 144, 149, 156
damp proofing 184
deeds 109, 110, 112
deposits 12, 25, 26, 28, 29, 112
  on exchange of contracts 29, 112
disputes 179–84
  with estate agents 97, 180
  with legal firms 181–2
  management 179–80
  with removal firms 183–4
  with sellers 183
  with surveyors 181
domestic energy assessors (DEAs) 106
downsizing 14, 59

electric checks 22, 149
electrical wiring and installations 92,
    149
employee mortgages 40
Energy Performance Certificates
    (EPCs) 105–7
equity 24, 28
estate agents 85, 93–102
  buying through 135–6
  choosing 95–9
  codes of practice 97
  complaints against 97, 180
  dealing with 21, 135
  fees and costs 93, 100, 101, 121, 180
  Ireland and Northern Ireland 197–
    8, 199, 202, 203
  joint/multiple agency 100–1
  key-handling policy 116
  mortgage arrangements 40, 121
  sale contract with 13, 17, 100–1
  Scotland 186
  selling through 17, 93–102

services and obligations 93–5,
    99, 102, 117, 122, 152, 159, 160
  sole agency 99, 100–1, 122
  tie-in periods 101
  valuations 86, 93, 96, 100
  and viewings 116
  withdrawing instructions from 122
exchange of contracts 13, 28, 101, 112,
    162, 164
  delays 162

failed sales, reasons for 105, 113, 121,
    124, 145, 160
Financial Conduct Authority (FCA)
    see Financial Services Authority
Financial Ombudsman Service (FOS)
    58
Financial Services Authority (FSA) 37,
    39, 50, 61
  change to Financial Conduct
    Authority (FCA) 25
first-time buyers 11–12, 15, 114, 118,
    139–42, 152, 173, 186
fixtures and fittings 91, 145, 183
fixtures and fittings form 110–11
flats and apartments 81, 150–1
  conveyancing 110
  cost of renewing a lease 151
flooding 64, 65, 82, 148
'For Sale' boards 93, 95, 103
fridges and freezers 170, 172, 174

gas checks 22, 149
gazumping 118, 160, 204
Green Deal 105–6
guaranteed treatments 111, 149, 178
  faulty 184
  transferable guarantees 184
guarantor 12

Halifax 78
Home Information Packs (HIPs) 105
  in Ireland 205
HomeBuy schemes 60, 139–41
Home Report 188, 191–2
Hometrack 77–8
house prices 74–5, 83–8, 94, 95, 134
house-hunting 135–8

housing associations 11, 12, 60, 62, 63, 140, 194

identity, proof of 22, 56, 110
income and expenditure 26–7, 34
income protection insurance 49
Incremental Purchase Scheme (Ireland) 202
independent financial advisers (IFAs) 24, 38, 40, 48, 51, 52, 57
see also mortgage lenders and intermediaries
insurance 64–72
  buildings and contents insurance 64–70, 92, 163
  higher lending charge 28, 30, 48
  life insurance 49
  for periods of accident, illness or unemployment 49, 61
  removals 163, 169
insurance company mortgages 40
internet 21–22
  initiatives 104
  mortgage information and deals 37, 56
  private and specialist property sites 136
  property price information 78, 85–6
Ireland 199–205
  advised minimum value (AMV) 199–200, 205
  buying a property 200–5
  estate agents 202, 203
  low-income buyers 202
  mortgages 202
  newly built houses 199, 200, 203
  property auctions 204
  selling your home 199–200
  stamp duty land tax (SDLT) 201
  surveys 205
  see also Northern Ireland

joint ownership 141–2
joint tenancy 91, 141–2

keys 94, 112, 164, 173, 174
  estate agents' key-handling policies 116

Land Registry 30, 76, 79, 110, 177, 196
Law Society 183
lease, cost of 151
leaseback, sale and 63
leasehold properties 30
  buildings insurance 66
  cost of renewing a lease 151
  ground rent (Northern Ireland) 196
  Ireland 204
  see also flats and apartments
life insurance 49
LIFT (Scotland) 194
light, natural 134
listed buildings 126, 127, 149–50
loans 11, 25, 29, 141
  bridging loans 47
  see also mortgage
local authorities
  mortgage scheme (Ireland) 202
locks 71
low-income buyers 60, 139–42
  Ireland 202
  Northern Ireland 197
  Scotland 194

mail redirection service 170, 172
maintenance, property 178
meter readings 170, 173, 174
missives (Scotland) 193
mortgage 36–63
  advice and information 24, 37, 56
  affordability 26, 33, 34, 35, 57
  application for 55, 56
  application rejection 59–60
  arrangement fees 28, 30, 48, 51
  cash back deals 45
  costs 22, 30, 47–8, 51, 54
  definition 36
  drawdown facility 46
  early repayment charges (redemption penalties) 45, 47–8, 55
  higher lending charge 28, 30, 48
  illness and unemployment 35
  interest rates 35, 36–7, 43–4, 54
  Ireland 202
  joint mortgages 11–12, 33, 141–2
  key facts illustration (KFI) 47, 48, 56

maximum loan 12, 29, 33, 59
mortgage rescue schemes 62
newly built houses 128
non-standard properties 61
overpayments 43, 55, 57
payment difficulties/arrears 55, 61–3
and the self-employed 32–3, 46–7, 59
term of the loan 41–2, 57, 62–3
unmarried couples 33
valuation for mortgage purposes 35,
    153
Mortgage Allowance Scheme (Ireland)
    203
mortgage lenders and intermediaries
    38, 50–1, 52–3
advised/non-advised service 50, 57
authorisation 52
banks 40, 51
brokers 38, 40, 48, 51, 52
builders 40, 128
building societies 37, 51
employers 40
estate agents 40, 121
fees 38, 48, 51, 52
initial disclosure document (IDD)
    51, 57
insurance companies 40
key questions to ask 52–5
mis-selling complaints 57, 58
Mortgage Agreement in Principle
    (MAP) 40, 55, 85, 94, 121, 160
regulation 38, 39, 50, 61
see independent financial
    advisers
mortgage types 42–5
base rate trackers 44
buy-to-let mortgages 47
capped rate deals 37, 44
combination deals 45
discounted-rate mortgages 44
fixed-rate mortgages 43
flexible (off-set) mortgages 45–6
interest-only mortgages 43, 53, 62
ISA mortgages 43
pension mortgages 43
portable mortgages 47, 48
repayment mortgages 42, 49
self-certification mortgage 46–7

standard variable rate (SVR)
    mortgages 43, 56
moving day 165–74
at the new home 173, 174
briefing sheet for new owner 171
d-i-y removal 166–7
essentials box 174
jobs before 166, 170–73
removals firm 166, 168–9
moving home
affordability 24–35, 57
alternatives to 14, 15, 16
costs 26, 28, 30–1
decision process 17–20
key phases 18–19
moving things along 20–1
reasons for 13–15
reasons not to move 15–16
timetable 16–17

National Association of Estate Agents
    (NAEA) 78–9, 98, 180
Nationwide 78
neighbourhood watch schemes 71
neighbours 111
NewBuy 140
newly built houses 11
buying off plan 127, 128, 129
conveyancing 110
defects 127, 129, 130, 203
environmental risks 149
guarantees 130, 198
Ireland 199, 200, 203
mortgages on 128
Northern Ireland 198
part exchange 40, 128, 138, 159
prices 129
pros and cons 126–9
self-build projects 130–2
newspapers 84–5
property advertisements 136
noise 133–4, 146, 150–1
Northern Ireland 196–8
Northern Ireland Co-Ownership
    Housing Association (NICHA) 197

offers
acceptance 118

offers (cont.)
  conditions 151
  gazumping 118, 160, 204
  making an offer 20, 22, 152
  negotiating 119, 152
  Scotland 189, 191, 192–3
  sealed bids 193
  vetting 118
Ombudsman schemes 97
Ombudsman Services: Property 97
Open Market Shared Equity Scheme
  194
open-plan houses 125

paperwork, organising 92, 176
park homes 142
period properties 12, 81, 126, 127
  see also listed buildings
permanent health insurance (PHI) 49
pets, moving 173
planning permission 13, 92, 132, 147
private property sales 102, 103–8, 122,
  136
private treaty (Ireland) 198, 200
property centres (Scotland) 186–7
property information form 110
property market 6–7, 9–12, 74–88
  crashes 78
  falling market 119, 155
  local market 79–82, 84–6
  prices and variations 74–9, 83–8, 94,
    95, 134
  strong market 119, 155
Property Misdescriptions Act 103
Property Ombudsman 97
Purchaser's Information Packs
  (Scotland) 188, 191, 192

radon 82, 149
recession, buying and selling during
  7–8
relocation services 137, 138
removals firms 166, 168–9
  access problems 168
  arranging date with 163
  briefing 169
  charges 31
  claims against 184

dispute with 183
  estimates 168–9
  insurance for the move 163, 169
  packing service 31, 168
  tipping 174
renovation 16
Rent-a-Room scheme (Ireland) 202
repossessions 138
Right to Acquire scheme 60
Right to Buy scheme 60
  Northern Ireland 197
  Scotland 194
Rightmove 76, 77
Royal Institute of Chartered
  Surveyors (RICS) 78, 94, 95, 98, 181
sales particulars 93, 103–4, 114, 120
savings and investments 25
school catchment areas 80, 81
Scotland 185–94
  buying a property 189–93
  entry date 187, 188, 193
  estate agents 186
  fixed and guideline prices 187, 188,
    190–1
  guaranteed treatments 184
  low-income buyers 142
  missives 193
  offers to buy 189, 191, 192–3
  Purchaser's Information Packs 188,
    191, 192
  sealed bids 193
  selling your home 186–8
  solicitors 186–7, 190
  stamp duty land tax 190
  surveys 187–8, 191–2
searches 13, 20, 30
security
  locks 71
  while selling your house 94, 115
self-build projects 130–2
  finding and buying land 131–2
  land survey 132
  planning permission 132
  professional services 132
self-employed people and mortgages
  32–3, 46–7, 59
selling your home 17–20, 89–122
  in an emergency 63

emotional issues 15, 90–1
failed sales, reasons for 113, 121,
    124, 145, 160
in a falling market 119
fixtures and fittings 91
Ireland 199–200
Northern Ireland 196
paperwork 92
preparing the house for sale 114–15
problems 120–2
sale by auction 137, 138
sales particulars 93, 103–4, 114, 120
Scotland 186–8
security factors 94, 115
in a strong market 119
through an estate agent 17–20,
    93–102
without an agent 103–8
see also conveyancing; HIPs; offers;
    viewings
services and costs disclosure
    document 51
shared equity 140
shared ownership 140–1
in Scotland 194
Social HomeBuy 60
solicitors and conveyancers
    choosing 108
    complaints against 181–2
    fees 22, 30, 108, 109, 110, 182
    instructing 109–10
    no sale, no fee 22, 109, 110
    Northern Ireland 198
    and property centres 186–7
    Scotland 186–7, 190
stamp duty land tax (SDLT) 22, 30, 31,
    176, 177, 178
    Ireland 202
    Northern Ireland 196–7
    payment 177
    rates 22, 177
    Scotland 190
state benefits and mortgage payments
    62
subsidence 70, 82, 148
surveyors 95
    complaints against 181
    estate agencies 94

'hidden defects' policy 181
surveys 28, 153–5, 178
    buildings survey 30, 156
    costs 30, 153, 156
    home condition report 147, 153,
        178, 181
    homebuyer report 30, 127, 154, 156
    Ireland 205
    land survey 132
    mortgage valuation 30, 153
    Northern Ireland 198
    poor surveys 121, 161
    Scotland 187–8, 191–2
    snagging 156

telephone 170
tenancy in common 142
thatched houses 29, 64
timber treatment 184
traffic noise and inconvenience 133,
    146

unmarried couples and mortgages 33
unwanted possessions, disposal of 91,
    166
utility services 92, 170, 172, 173

valuations 86–8
    by the estate agent 86, 93, 96, 100
    high valuations 86
    low valuations 35
    for mortgage purposes 35, 153
    price per square metre 87, 88, 146
    property comparison 86, 87
viewings 94, 116–18, 136, 143–6
    checklist 143, 146
    no viewings 120
    open days 116
    preparing your home 114–15
    questions to ask 145

wills 178
working from home 64

Which? is the largest independent consumer organisation in the UK. A not-for-profit organisation, we exist to make individuals as powerful as the organisations they deal with in everyday life. Our campaigns make people's lives fairer, simpler and safer. The next few pages give you a taster of our many products and services. For more information, log onto www.which.co.uk or call 01992 822800.

Which? Online and Which? Local

www.which.co.uk gives you access to all Which? content online and much, much more. It's updated regularly, so you can read hundreds of product reports and Best Buy recommendations, keep up to date with Which? campaigns, compare products, use our financial planning tools and search for the best cars on the market. As a Which? member you can sign up to Which? Local, a website of 110,000 local business reviews created for Which? members, by Which? members. Covering everything from plumbers to plasterers and butchers to bakers, our independent member reviews will help you find the best service that won't charge you over the odds. To subscribe, go to www.which.co.uk.

Which? Legal Service

Which? Legal Service offers convenient access to first-class legal advice at unrivalled value. One low-cost annual subscription enables members to receive tailor-made legal advice by telephone or email on a wide variety of legal topics, including consumer law – problems with goods and services, employment law (for employees), holiday problems, neighbour disputes, parking tickets and Wills and Probate Administration in England and Wales. To subscribe, call the Members' helpline: 01992 822828 or go to www.whichlegalservice.co.uk.

Which? Money

Whether you want to boost your pension, make your savings work harder or simply need to find the best credit card, *Which? Money* has the information you need. *Which? Money* offers you honest, unbiased reviews of the best (and worst) personal finance deals, from bank accounts to loans, credit cards to savings accounts. It's also packed with investigations, revealing the truth behind the small print, and letting you know which financial companies you can trust. To subscribe, go to www.which.co.uk/publications/magazines/which-money/.

Other books in this series

Which? Books

Which? Books provide impartial, expert advice on everyday matters from finance and law to gardening, property and major life events. We also publish the country's most trusted restaurant guide, *The Good Food Guide*. To find out more about Which? Books, log on to www.which.co.uk or call 01903 828 557.

'Which? tackles the issues that really matter to consumers and gives you the advice and active support you need to buy the right products.'

Renting and Letting

Kate Faulkner
ISBN 978 1 84490 116 6
Price £10.99

A practical guide for landlords, tenants and anybody considering the buy-to-let market. Written by an experienced property professional, this real-world guide covers all the legal and financial matters, including tax, record-keeping and mortgages, as well as disputes, deposits and security.

Develop Your Property

Kate Faulkner
ISBN 978 1 84490 038 1
Price £10.99

Develop Your Property helps add value to your property by guiding you through the processes of extension, renovation and conversion. Learn how to budget and project-manage building work and implement key property changes that can add real value. Includes valuable information on planning permission, building regulations and getting the builders in.

Which? Mortgage Advisers

Are you buying your first home, moving to a new one, or reviewing your current mortgage deal? If so, we can help.

Which? Mortgage Advisers will search through all the options to help you find the mortgage that's right for you.

Many mortgage advisers only consider mortgages that they can arrange for you, but *Which? Mortgage Advisers* look at every mortgage from every available lender. This includes those that you can only get directly from banks and building societies.

Our advisers take time to listen to what you want so that they can truly understand your circumstances and needs. They don't receive any personal commission, so the only reason for recommending a mortgage is that they think it's right for you.

Five reasons to choose Which? Mortgage Advisers:

■ Impartial advice from a qualified adviser who's looking out for your best interests
■ Advice that is based on looking at every mortgage from every available lender
■ Straightforward, jargon-free advice that makes sense
■ Great service that saves you time and hassle
■ Advice that you don't need to pay for*

To find out more – with no obligation whatsoever – call us today on 0800 197 7219 or visit **www.whichmortgageadvisers.co.uk**

*administrative fee of £99 payable at the point of application should you decide to proceed with our recommendation

Your home may be repossessed if you do not keep up repayments on your mortgage.

Which? Mortgage Advisers is a trading name of Which? Financial Services Limited, part of the Which? Group. Which? Financial Services Ltd, Registered Office: 2 Marylebone Road, London NW1 4DF. Registered in England and Wales No. 7239342. Which? Financial Services Ltd is authorised and regulated by the Financial Services Authority (No. 527029). Telephone calls may be recorded and/ or monitored. We do not charge for mortgage advice however, should we help you proceed with your mortgage there is an administrative fee of £99 payable at the point of application. Should you wish to pay us a fee for the mortgage advice, we will charge a fee of 0.5% of the loan, payable on completion and if we receive any commission for your transaction we will refund this to you.